WHEN LIGHT PIERCED THE DARKNESS

A Former NASA Engineer's Extraordinary Story Of Redemption

Richard E. Herskind

WHEN LIGHT PIERCED THE DARKNESS
A Former NASA Engineer's Extraordinary Story Of Redemption

by Richard E. Herskind

ISBN: 978-1-935018-42-1

Copyright ©2016 by Richard E. Herskind

Published by:

5 Stones Publishing

All rights reserved.

Interior Design: Leo Ward

Editor: Ann Van De Water

Special thanks to: Gina Detwiler and Sharon Claassen for their helpful editing suggestions and the flow of the story.

For additional copies of this book, please contact the author Richard E. Herskind at: piercinglightmemoir@gmail.com

Dedication

To my loving wife Kathy; my faithful life companion, and helpmate along the way.

TABLE OF CONTENTS

FROM THE AUTHOR

Everyone has a story. I have been encouraged to write this memoir because many have said, "Your story could be an encouragement to others, write it up some day." That day has come, and what follows is my story.

I have written this memoir to give encouragement to many who are seeking a genuine relationship with Jesus Christ and followers of Jesus who are reticent to share their faith with friends and colleagues especially in the workplace. Much of Jesus' ministry of healing and hope was carried out in the workplace of his day. People with whom we work and spend most of our days are looking for light in their personal darkness. Jesus said to his followers;

> *"Here's another way to put it: you're here to be light, bringing out the God-colors in the world. God is not a secret to be kept. We're going public with this, as public as a city on a hill. If I make you light-bearers, you don't think I'm going to hide you under a bucket, do you? I'm putting you on a light stand. Now that I've put you there on a hilltop, on a light stand—shine! Keep open house; be generous with your lives. By opening up to others, you'll prompt people to open up with God, this generous Father in heaven" (Matt. 5:15-16 [The Message]).*

My story is one of new beginnings and unexpected turns. It is a story of intense suffering and extraordinary healing. It is a story that is spiritual at its core, and transformational in daily life. It is also an incomplete story; the events of the earlier part of my life.

It is my desire that some who read on will find inspiration and hope for their lives. Miraculous possibilities exist when pursued through the eyes of faith. Extraordinary living is demonstrated in the pages of the Hebrew-Christian Scriptures, which tell of the life, death and resurrection of Jesus Christ.

Were it not for the many people with whom I have worked and associated with over the years, this story could not have been written. I have changed the names of many, while telling the stories of my interaction with them as accurately as possible. Some of these people have passed on from this life. However, I believe they all had an encounter with the possibilities of new life while laboring daily in the workplace.

1

AN ASSAULT FROM THE DARK SIDE

At the age of eighteen I experienced a world of emotional and mental pain similar to what many of our soldiers experience when they return from war, although I can't be certain. I was in the military at the time, had volunteered to serve in the US Army, was trained by the military police, and served stateside without firing a shot at an enemy or receiving enemy fire. The internal conflict however was intense. It involved an enemy that could not be seen, was far advanced in deception and cruelty, and demonstrated a resolve to destroy. I learned of my condition slowly and painfully in a military hospital to which I was admitted. I invite you to walk this journey with me and learn how it impacted my life and the lives of many others.

> *"For our struggle is not against flesh and blood, but against the rulers, against the authorities, against the powers of this dark world and against the spiritual forces of evil in the heavenly realms" (Eph. 6:12[NIV]).*

SOMETHING IS WRONG!

The doctor excused himself, backed his chair away from his desk and walked toward the door. In his momentary absence, my curiosity demanded to know what he had written in my file. I stretched my neck squinting to read upside down and managed to notice a box in the lower right corner of the open page. It was titled "Preliminary Diagnosis". What I saw next brought a lump to my throat. Were my eyes deceiving me? Approaching footsteps outside the door signaled his imminent return. I quickly assumed my "waiting" posture as he opened the door, hoping he hadn't noticed.

"Private Herskind, I am recommending that you stay here in the hospital facilities over the weekend." Lt. Colonel Dr. Benjamin Alcott, Psychiatrist at the US Army Hospital at Fort Hood Texas, adjusted his glasses and placed a call to the admissions office to request a room for me for the weekend. I muttered to myself that something was very wrong. Perhaps the previous tests were not conclusive and he was having second thoughts. Then again, perhaps a few more tests would clear things up.

What kind of room was he requesting? I was confused. On the one hand was fear of the unknown; on the other hand, just maybe there was hope for me. I wanted to believe the latter.

A staff aide appeared and accompanied me to my weekend accommodation. The silent stares of other patients, some secured to their rooms, followed us as we walked, while my mind created a mental picture of what my "weekend home" might look like.

A hospital gown and footwear were provided in exchange for my Army uniform, the return of which was promised for Monday. As we approached our destination the aide reached in his pocket for his set of keys and opened the iron barred security door in front me. As I crossed over into the room, my eyes scanned left to right. I noticed a single bed, a small table and chair, the only furnishings in the room. A small iron-barred window, out of reach, located on the upper back wall provided the only source of natural light. The door to the room was, like the others I had seen, designed with security in mind, presumably to prevent unattended wanderings throughout the facility. With the door secured, the footsteps of my escort slowly faded as he walked down the hallway. A strange and eerie silence filled my room.

I sat motionless on the hard bed, somewhat relieved despite a day filled with confusion and uncertainty. However it was short-lived as loneliness and fear took my mind hostage. I became aware of an unseen presence accusing and condemning me, as if carrying out some higher orders.

The light outside peering through the window in the upper back wall slowly gave way to a single glaring light bulb attached to the ceiling. Questions flooded my mind, such as: "How did I get here? What had my life become, how long will I be here, and why this inner fear and turmoil?" I looked within for answers, but found none. The thought of God entered my mind, but what would He have to do with me anyway? I had refused His overtures as a young teenager.

Unwelcome noises echoed through the hallway, punctuating the night, and feeding my fears. Monday could not come fast enough. I yearned for Monday. The clock in the hallway seemed to have slowed, changing minutes into hours. I could not imagine what lay ahead. In my solitude, I began to rehearse the past, searching for an explanation of how events in my life might have led to these temporary quarters for the weekend.

OF TWO MINDS

"... Do not waver, for a person with divided loyalty is as unsettled as a wave of the sea that is blown and tossed by the wind. Such people should not expect to receive anything from the Lord. Their loyalty is di-

vided between God and the world, and they are unstable in everything they do" (Jas. 1:6-8 [NLT]).

I was raised in suburban Boston, Massachusetts. I was the first born, followed by a sister, a brother and another sister. My parents planted within each of us the values of love, honesty, obedience, a respect for authority, and an appreciation for service to others motivated by faith.

Life in the church was a central part of our family and home. The Bible was the most respected and treasured book. Memories of Dad giving himself to the service of those who were very much less fortunate than us were imprinted on my young mind. His faith based radio broadcast "Uncle Elmer's Song Circle" created an imaginary "church" in an imaginary town called Pleasantville. The church featured a 20 voice choir broadcasting live from the studio. Many of his radio listeners were invalids, and for them, attending "church" on Sunday morning was to tune into Uncle Elmer's Song Circle on station WHDH in Boston. In time, invitations were extended to Dad to bring his radio choir from the studio to various churches across New England where he shared the gospel.

During the week Dad worked hard at providing the poor with items from radios to wheelchairs that his audience had donated. We children grew up never realizing that we were not far from being poor ourselves.

One imprint on my young heart was the level of faith I saw in my Dad. One cold winter, our coal bin was nearly empty. I asked Dad when the coal man was coming. He said "Soon." What I didn't know was that Dad had no money to pay for any coal, and yet he trusted that God would provide when the time came. The day before the scheduled delivery, a letter came in the mail from a radio listener with a check and a note inside. The note explained that my Dad was to use the money only for his family and not for the ministry. As Dad was serving others, God had placed others to serve our family. The money allowed a full bin of coal with some money left over for other family needs.

Church and faith helped shape my youthful view of myself and the world. I was single-minded, believing the Bible's message of God's love and concern for all human beings. The central message we learned as children was the forgiveness of sin through the death and resurrection of Jesus. However, in me, that childlike faith would soon conflict with the values and behavior of those who had become my friends in elementary and high school.

Mom was the nurturer in our home, and Dad, the disciplinarian. Both parents were motivated by love. Dad's discipline was sincerely what he thought was right, yet I seldom felt that I could please him. He had high expectations of me, the first born. I can still hear him say some version of the following: "Son, to be successful in life you have to work hard, study hard, and learn self discipline." Dad was an example of what he was expecting of me. However, as I moved from grade to grade in school, my interest in learning waned, and my report card was showing the effects. "Son, you can do better than that!" If I got a "C" he would say, "You know, with a little more effort you can get a 'B'." If it was a "B", I would be reminded that teachers also give "A's". Inwardly I wanted to please him. I knew he was right. In many ways Dad affirmed me, and I had deep respect for the reflection of his faith in service to others. However, I felt a conflict arising within, a conflict that would grow in time.

My adolescent world was shaken in the fifth grade. One day while walking across the playground on my way home from school, I was assaulted by a pack of bullies. The three were notorious for picking fights with those who looked vulnerable and unable to defend themselves. I can still hear in their laughter, their recognition of my fear as they approached me. Encircling my space they growled, "Hey, where are you going boy? Home to mama?" The biggest of the three lunged at me and threw me to the ground. In response to the laughter and mocking of his cohorts, he proceeded to demonstrate his worthiness as their leader by planting his knee forcefully on my face leaving me with a bloodied nose and shirt. Laughter, mocking and threats of more to come in the future left me feeling terrified and very much alone and hurting.

I went home confused and ashamed to face Mom and Dad who I thought might assume that I had provoked the attack. However, one look at me generated concern and consolation even though I feared divulging who had assaulted me. What role did this experience have on my psyche? Did it cause me to strive, in the wrong way, to be accepted by pleasing my peers? Was that experience among the reasons I was sitting in these weekend accommodations in a psychiatric hospital beginning to loathe myself?

In junior and senior high school, I had a deepening need for peer acceptance and became willing to betray the values which I had inherited. It seemed strange, but there was a new excitement in pursuing things I knew were wrong. As a seventh grader, sneaking behind the school building for a borrowed cigarette was exhilarating and frightening; exhilarating because it provided me with acceptance by my peers, and frightening because I might be caught by the school authorities and sent home with a disciplinary note. The promise of peer acceptance came with a price. The road to a cigarette addiction started behind the school that day, and dogged me for several years. Had drugs and pornography been readily available in those days, I might have succumbed to them as well. Alcohol was available but I never acquired a taste for it, unlike some of my friends.

Wanting to be accepted by peers was a costly, one-sided and losing proposition. Was my current state of mind somehow related to a deep need of peer acceptance, and a need to be significant among others in order to find personal meaning in my life? Does everybody go through this? It didn't seem to relate to the confusion I had as I sat on that hard bed behind a locked door I could not open. There was a growing sense of a more significant reason.

AN OFFER REFUSED

Growing up in a home where faith and the church played a significant role in our family's social and spiritual life, expectations were placed on me and my siblings. It was understood, for example, that we would be at every meeting of our church youth group. One evening, while listening to a visiting youth pastor, I had a most unexpected experience. As I sat contemplating his words, I heard a small whisper seemingly over my right shoulder. "My Son, I know what you are looking for. Let me into your life, and I will give you a life worth living".

Somehow I knew that the intruding voice was the voice of God's Spirit, even though I had never heard it before. My quick, angry and defiant response to that inner voice surprised me. I said "No! Maybe when I am forty or fifty years old we can talk again!" I would not recognize, until much later, that some apparently random and insignificant statements spoken to one's self can be life changing. I was betting that evening that I could live with inner contradictions. I did not understand however, that I had given my life over to the authority of the enemy of all human beings. I had given allegiance to forces unseen. However, like a chameleon, I reasoned I could still fit in with the church youth and act as though I was one of them whenever I was with them.

I was now of two minds. I had embraced two incompatible and opposite world views. One allowed me to live in the present world with its promises of finding life in its pleasures. The other was the world in which I had been nurtured from childhood, a life of faith and trust in Him who had created me. It seemed logical that I did not have to abandon the belief formed in childhood; it would just be inactive while I tasted the fruit of the more available one. "You can switch over to the other at a later time" said the impostor who had slithered into my mind.

From that night on, I had one set of friends at the church who knew me as one of them, a "Christian" and a fellow "confirmand". The other set of friends were in the world at school, and they knew me as one of them; an image seeker willing to use their salty language and push the rebellious envelope to gain their approval. However, living two lives required that I keep up my guard. God forbid that I would be together in the same room at the same time with both sets of friends. Surely my cover of posing as a Christian while being fully committed to a world of hypocrisy would eventually be blown.

Shortly after graduating from high school, my high school sweetheart Joann and I discussed becoming engaged to be married. I didn't give much thought to related questions I would have to face sooner or later. Questions like what kind of work would I be doing to support a wife and family? I had no money, no marketable skills, and college was unthinkable. However, a temporary solution—which could put a wedding off for a few years—was to get my military obligation out of the way. I could buy time by volunteering for the draft, which was hanging over me anyway. After talking it over, we decided that in the fall of our graduation year, I would say goodbye to friends, family and my future wife, and answer the call of Uncle Sam.

THE MAKING OF A SOLDIER

I raised my right hand, took the oath of a private in the US Army and boarded a train in Boston, Massachusetts destined for basic training at Fort Dix, New Jersey. I had no clue about what difficulties lay ahead, and little did I know that I was about to learn some things that would expose what was going on inside me.

I soon discovered that the rules of the military are created in another universe; the universe of discipline, obedience to superiors, and competency in one's MOS (major occupation specialty). Civilian life and the life of a soldier are governed by two totally different sets of rules. The goal of military training at its core is the transformation of attitude, loyalty and obedience to a higher authority. Those with that authority wore certain insignias on their arms or bars on their shoulders.

Shining boots, making a bed the army way, and how to clean and fire a weapon were among the basic physical skills to be learned. But more important were those challenges to the will, mind and emotions. Being verbally assaulted by a master sergeant began the process. I quickly had an "issue" with my superiors telling me what to do and when to do it, including eating, sleeping and training. To acknowledge such authority seemed a little much for my undisciplined spirit.

One night, while sound asleep with about fifty other recruits, an intoxicated sergeant burst into the barracks. It was about 2:00 a.m., and there he was, barking irritating commands along the lines of "Awright, listen up! Attention! I said attennnnnntion!

Get out of those bunks, come on, mooove it!" The slur in his voice suggested that we might ignore him. However, the fear of raw authority made that thought short-lived. He continued, "I said, out of your bunks! Full field packs, boots, get your weapons on the way out, fall in formation at the front of the barracks." Ironically, he was screaming "Be quiet; don't wake your buddies next door! You have 7 minutes! Come on, come on, haven't got much time, move it, move it!!!!"

In obedience we were, in fact, standing in formation in the time allotted. Now we waited to hear what else he had to say. The freezing cold New Jersey winter morning was not pleasant!

Outside, the sergeant continued his tirade. "The current temperature is 20 degrees. The sky is clear and you can see that the good Lord has provided us with a bright moon to light our path. We are headed 8 miles north of here to attack an enemy outpost that has settled there. Follow me!" he barked. The sergeant then got into a warmed Jeep, where he continued criticizing our attitude, yelling obscenities describing and mocking our weaknesses as "wanna-be" soldiers. Shivering in the cold with rifles on our shoulders, and keeping in step by singing marching songs was not my idea of anything beneficial, either in mind, body or spirit!

Hours into our march, and with a tangible hatred for that jerk who was riding along in his warm jeep barking at us, I began to detect a subtle mood change within me. It was totally unexpected and took me by surprise. I looked up at the moon and said to myself, "Wow, hey, this is great! I love this!" There was a new determination in my steps and the rhythm of boots marching together became a pleasant sound. The marching songs added to a sense of purpose, a building of unity amongst us. We were becoming a band of brothers. I was becoming a soldier and loving it!

Strangely, I willingly yielded to the one barking commands from his warm jeep. I yielded to the notion of someone over me commanding obedience, demanding that I enter the cold winter evening for an eight mile march to meet and destroy the "imaginary" enemy. In a strange way it was a satisfying state of mind. I became compliant in every way. I became an obedient soldier committed to carrying out my leader's commands. And yes, I had come to serve our nation. Call me an obedient soldier of Company C, ready to take on the enemy. Well not quite yet! However, a big training objective had been accomplished in "breaking" this recruit.

What this meant in the overall scheme of things was to unfold in the days ahead. I was separated from my civilian ways and passed the first test of training --obedience and submission to authority. Additional discipline and training with a team of infantry warriors, qualified me for advanced training at Fort Gordon, Georgia where I would learn the discipline and skills required in a

Trained as an MP

military police unit. That in turn led me to a permanent assignment to a military police company in Fort Hood, Texas where my duties included continued readiness training and guarding security facilities. I had settled in as a soldier, learned respect for authority and was willing to work hard as an MP. But not all was well.

THE DARK SHADOW LENGTHENS

Further training allowed me to wear the MP arm band of the Military Police. I now had the authority and power that goes along with being a member of a Military Police unit. However, the illusion of having a position of power and authority was about to be challenged.

The challenge came from an unexpected event. I received a letter from Joann, the girl I planned to marry. Mixed in with news about home, she shared that she had gone to a party where some of my high school buddies were also in attendance. I felt a deep emotional pain as I read, and began to question why she chose to party with people I did not fully trust.

I put the letter down, and then picked it up to read it over and over again for several days. I had a hard time sleeping. Fear became an unwelcome companion. I became obsessed, thinking of what might have happened at that party. That I was projecting my own hypocrisy on my girlfriend didn't matter. The unthinkable began to torture me.

Shortly thereafter, while passing the door to the chaplain's office, I noticed it was open. Perhaps he could help this confused soldier. But why was I interested in talking to a chaplain since God and I were on hold? It didn't matter. Perhaps the chaplain, being a counselor, could help me sort out my thoughts. After listening to my concerns, he said "Private Herskind is Fort Hood your first assignment following basic and MP training?" I told him it was. I also told him I wasn't getting any sleep and it was affecting my work. Then, he got "spiritual" with me and suggested that I just trust God with my concerns. He told me there are many adjustments to be made in the military. "Give yourself some time, and things will turn around for you." I nodded my head and thanked him for his time, stood up, and left his office agitated with unexplained anger. Again, why I even went into his office was not clear. I certainly didn't want a lecture about God; I only wanted help in seeking relief from my sleepless nights.

The lack of sleep was weighing heavily on me. I needed to give full attention to my job, and became concerned that I might mess up through a lack of focus. I decided to seek some additional help from the medical staff. Surely they would have an answer for this insomnia issue.

The medical doctor with whom I spoke had a silver leaf on his collar, evidence of the rank of Lt. Colonel. I tried to explain what was going on in my mind and told him about the letter I received from my girlfriend back home. I admitted to him that I was probably reading into the letter and that I was only imagining what might have taken place at that party. I cannot recall much of the conversation that followed, but the doctor wrote a prescription for some "sleeping aids" which was an encouragement since that was why I was seeing him in the first place. He told me I could see him again if sleeping was still a problem.

As I stood to leave, he made a curious and unexpected comment. "It sounds to me, Private Herskind, like you have lost your faith in God." Did I say something that caused him to say that? I don't recall. Was he a Christian? In any case, his statement hit me like a bolt of lightning. God hadn't been part of our conversation and to me it seemed right out of the blue. I looked at him and with an unexplained surge of anger, turned and exited the door slamming it shut. I immediately got concerned inwardly, believing that my arrogant response could have landed me in big trouble since I had shown disrespect toward an officer. I left the building quickly.

While walking back to my unit and still angry, I noticed a small dark cloud in an otherwise cloudless expanse on the horizon. Then I heard this in my spirit: "There is a great storm on the way." Inwardly I felt I was being informed of terrible things to come; that what started small would soon overtake me in a violent and merciless way. I made my way to the base pharmacy to get my prescription filled. The "relaxing pills" and the "sleep medication" had no effect. I even overdosed on the evening medication, drinking half of a bottle, thinking it would be more effective. Again there was no effect. It may have been a placebo designed to "suggest" sleep more than cause it.

I returned to the doctor, and while apologizing for my abrupt departure the week before, requested to see a psychiatrist. After asking some additional questions and gathering information that would accompany his referral, he contacted the psychiatric unit of the hospital on base and arranged for an appointment. I thanked him and left his office.

After some preliminary visits, psychological tests and information gathering, the psychiatrist, Lt. Col. Dr. Benjamin Alcott, arranged that I spend a weekend at the hospital facility. So there I sat alone in this room, secured by a door with iron reinforcements, full of unanswered questions and fear my constant companion.

THE BREAKING OF THE WILL AND SUBMISSION TO AUTHORITY

As I sat alone in my cell, I reflected on my experience at boot camp and Military Police training. I could see the training rationale for "breaking me" and transferring my allegiance to those over me in authority. It was painful, but it was effective, and gave me the mind of a soldier; one who had learned obedience to those over me in authority.

But now in the quietness of this room, I realized the possibility of a bigger authority problem; this time with God, Creator of the universe, the highest of all authorities (Rom. 13:1-2). My double life was evidence that I had acted in rebellion and arrogance toward God. While I had acknowledged Him as a child, I had the audacity to tell Him to get out of my life as a teenager. I told Him I did not want Him interfering with my plans. I proclaimed that I knew best concerning my life, and it was the highest expression of human rebellion.

Spiritually, I was not aware that being a human being I had a natural attitude of rebellion toward God. The prophet Samuel had spoken centuries earlier about the seriousness of rebellion when he said,

> *"For rebellion is like the sin of divination, and arrogance like the evil of idolatry...."(1 Sam. 15:23 [NIV]).*

I sat in silence on my bed, waiting for the arrival of Monday morning. I was beginning to feel a divine rejection that was heavy and tangible. It became all consuming. Nothing mattered except finding my way out of this descent into what I feared was a personal hell. I felt like God had become that barking commander. I also believed that His authority was the greatest of all, and that rebellion was deeply rooted in my soul.

THE DESCENT INTO DARKNESS

I could not erase from my mind what I saw in Dr. Alcott's office when I stole a peek at his hand written note suggesting a preliminary diagnosis of "possible schizophrenia." I knew nothing about this condition, but fear made it feel like a death sentence.

Later in the morning, Dr. Alcott entered my room, shook my hand and asked me how I was doing. I asked him if Monday was still the day I would be released back to my MP unit. His answer caused me concern. He informed me that an additional week was planned for observations by a staff of doctors, nurses and other support personnel. The purpose was to establish procedures and a treatment plan that would benefit me. Monday apparently was not to be my release day.

A routine was established making each day like the day before. In the morning a nurse would come by with medication and take routine measurements of my vital signs. It appeared to me that medications were always changing, sometimes in the form of pills different in color and shape, and at other times in a liquid form. I began to hope in each pill each day but there was no change. I asked for information on my condition, but it was not forthcoming except for an assurance that the doctor would soon explain the plan for my care.

Finally Dr. Alcott informed me that I would be involved in a patient assessment session. On the morning of the session, a nurse walked me to a large conference room. I noticed many chairs, placed in a large circle where staff members and other nurses and doctors were already seated. My chair was in the center of the circle. Dr. Alcott explained that the purpose of the meeting was to form a strategy going forward which would lead to a successful resolution of my internal struggle. I felt very much alone.

At the meeting I was asked many questions including questions about my relationship with God. How did I feel about Him? How did I feel He felt about me? Was I hearing voices? I had to acknowledge that, yes, I did hear some voices. I would learn much later that hearing voices was often a symptom of schizophrenia. A summary of the results from the meeting including the establishment of a treatment plan to be carried out over several weeks was communicated to me by Dr. Alcott.

ALL HELL MAKES AN ASSAULT

A few days later, Dr. Alcott came to my cell to tell me about the treatment plan. It included a procedure called Electro Convulsive Therapy (ECT) or Electro-Shock Therapy. He seemed confident and believed that, in time, I would experience the relief I desired. With his white lab coat and a stethoscope around his neck he explained the process that would be used. I learned to trust him because I believed that he was genuinely concerned for my welfare. Placing my faith in him, I agreed to go ahead with a series of those treatments which started several days later.

A nurse visited me at 6:00 a.m. on the day of the first treatment and gave me a pill presumably to decrease anxiety. The treatment was scheduled for 9:00 a.m..

The trip to the treatment room was by wheel chair. As we passed other patient's cells along the way, I recognized some of the residents from the day I was admitted to the facility. I wondered what they were thinking. Had they taken this trip to the ECT room? What did they know that I would soon find out? I had an eerie sense of being a condemned man on the way to his death. When we arrived at the treatment room fear mocked me at the door.

A round light hanging from a chain placed a large spot of light on the long table on which I would be laying. Not having any understanding of how ECT worked gave me the feeling that I was an experimental object at the mercy of the medical community. Daily medications were not working so I assumed that

I needed a more potent approach. Was it standard procedure? I didn't know.

Next to the long table, was another shorter table with pieces of electronic equipment including multiple cables which would presumably be attached to my body. When the wheelchair reached the long table, I was instructed to stand and step on the small stool with my back to the table. Aides helped me swing my legs lengthwise on the table so I could lie on my back. The table had a thin mattress which was not very comfortable and a small pillow to support my head.

I lay on the table paralyzed with fear. As the doctor and staff was busy preparing, I felt I had given permission for them to do horrible things to me. With the attachment of the wires to my body I sensed that I was being prepared for the worst. Was there no one to defend me? The weight of condemnation on my soul was the absence and silence of God who had honored my request to get out of my life.

Despite God's distance and the feeling that He would not hear, I felt an urgent need to pray. Would He be merciful in my last hour? If He really cared, surely He would come to my aid. I tried to pray. I quickly clasped my hands, pressing my palms together. As I began to pray, my mind suddenly filled with screaming voices, spouting the vilest words. Condemning voices broadcasted shouts of four-letter words to assault me. A stream of mocking filth taunted my mind mercilessly. It was hell unleashed. I unclasped my hands to stop the assault.

Still desperate, I tried again to pray, but the shrill voices lurking in my mind exploded once again determined to block me from any response from God whom I desperately wanted to hear. I deeply regretted the day I told God to get out of my life until I was ready to receive Him.

I lay limp on the table. Inwardly, agonizing tears poured into my broken soul. I could only wait for my destruction minutes away. The technicians finished their work of wiring me to the electronic device. The anesthesiologist started the drip of medication into my left arm. He attempted to comfort me with assurance that the medication would put me to sleep in a few minutes.

The medication began taking effect. My motor reflexes started to fail, leaving me unable to raise my arms, or move my legs or any other part of my body. I became totally immobilized, and could not have signaled the doctors for any reason, although I could hear their conversation very clearly. The panic within increased. I thought that by now I should have been unconscious. The effectiveness of the medication seemed to have reached its maximum and yet I could still hear what was going on around me. I struggled to breathe but my lungs didn't work. I became desperate to breathe. Suffocation was overtaking me. I wanted to object but could not indicate my distress with any part of my body. Finally, an oxygen mask was placed across my mouth and nose and air was pumped into my lungs. The rush of oxygen was a moment of relief.

One of the staff asked: "Is the patient asleep?" Still conscious and hearing their conversation, I cried out inside my paralyzed body screaming "NO, NO! STOP! I AM NOT ASLEEP!" Then, a jolt of electricity was released. I felt the whole thing.

It was a most violent physical attack; like a jack-hammer breaking through cement or highway road construction, or like a thunderbolt of electricity passing from one side of my head to the other. Mercifully the treatment knocked me out. I don't know if there were any additional shocks on this first occasion. When consciousness returned I found myself in a recovery room with four strong men standing over me.

My response upon wakening was violent. My instinct was irrational. I felt I had to escape the facility, wake up from this nightmare, get my military clothes and go back to a normal life with my military unit. It took the aides several minutes to wrestle me into submission. Totally exhausted, I collapsed and was wheeled back to my cell.

For several weeks, suicidal thoughts stalked my mind. It appeared that demonic forces were upping the ante as time went on. The initial treatment was followed by ten others over the next few months. Mercifully however an increase in the sodium pentathol medication rendered me unconscious in subsequent treatments sparing the pain but not the fear of the first treatment. I became convinced that my life was coming to an end.

THE ENEMY FULLY EXPOSED

In the days and evenings of weeks to come, I was plagued with the growing conviction that I was being mentally manipulated and decimated in a systematic way beyond my control. I was constantly listening to reasoning designed to reduce me to a human being not worthy of living. Self-condemnation went so deep it led me to believe that such thoughts were my own. Yet because I did not want these accusations, I wondered if my thoughts were being reported to me by a surrogate impostor, skillful beyond anything rational. The character of those "voices" I heard at my first treatment when I tried to pray, exposed the source of that deception, though I did not see the connection immediately. Because of this, I sent for the Bible my parents had given me as a going away gift upon entering the military.

I sought the Bible as medication, to get some comfort in my pain. However, as I read, there was constant opposition. I noticed that any passage of scripture that held out hope, was immediately attacked by the voices within, causing me to conclude that Biblical encouragement was for others, but not for me. My time had passed. My destiny was now certain; there was no hope. In fact virtually every scripture which expressed hope was an inner occasion for demonic mocking and condemnation.

Reading the Bible was painful and I had a sense that God had become to me the angry Master Sergeant who tried to break me from my civilian ways and transform me into an obedient soldier in the military. Was I now listening to a condemning voice of God, declaring how weak, inadequate and useless I was? Was I now on another kind of midnight march never to return?

On Good Friday evening of Easter weekend, I was lying in bed trying to rest when I felt the amassing of a great number of voices around my bed. They spoke, laughed, condemned me, and told me that there was no hope and no escape. My death was imminent. Unable to talk, I placed my hands on my stomach to check my breathing and prove to myself and those voices that I was still alive. The voices mocked again. I lay in bed wondering if I would ever see the light of a new day.

Saturday of Easter weekend was a blur. I placed several "collect" long distance calls to home, and could hear in my parents' voices the grief of not being able to be with their son in such hopeless circumstances. I asked for prayer and God's mercy. They assured me that many were praying.

On Easter Sunday at 1:00 pm, a television was unexpectedly delivered to my cell by one of Dr. Alcott's staff, or so I presumed. It was out of my reach on the other side of the iron barred door. I could not touch it, change the channel, or adjust it in any way. Between 1:00 and 2:00 p.m., I watched a film portraying the Passion of the Crucifixion of Jesus Christ. I was very familiar with this historical event and could have narrated it as it unfolded. I had believed it as a youth, and with fear I believed it now.

In the film, after the decision of the Roman authorities to crucify Jesus, He was strapped to a flogging post. Mocking and jeering could be heard in the background as the whips tore into the flesh of this accused renegade. I became a passive unconcerned observer, a bystander watching alongside the executioners who had directed many such floggings in the past. As the film progressed however, something was stirring deep within. I began to take an active interest in the drama. In spirit, I became one with the crowd, celebrating and calling for the crucifixion of Jesus. The inner voices in my mind aligned me against Jesus and put thoughts of increasing anger, rage, and bitterness deep within my mind and heart.

When Jesus had been delivered to the place of crucifixion, the Roman soldiers in charge placed his bloodied body against the wooden cross, which lay on the ground. I found myself participating in the drama, like being transported into the very scene I was watching. I grabbed a hammer and energized by the emotions of hatred, I joined the soldiers as they fastened Jesus to the cross. While driving nails into Jesus' hands and feet I cried out, "Jesus you have ruined my life!" Then, exhausted, I dropped the hammer to watch as the soldiers lifted the cross on which Jesus hung, placing it between two thieves.

I began weeping uncontrollably with agonizing sorrow for having rejected Him earlier in my young teens. As the film progressed, the camera angle placed the viewer at the foot of the cross looking up into Jesus' face. Then I heard Jesus speak words I had heard many times before; He said, "Father, forgive them, for they do not know what they are doing" (Luke 23:34). I fell to my knees as though at the cross and looked into His face, and cried out, "Jesus, I am one of them. I did not know what I was doing. Have mercy, forgive me, I cannot go on unless you raise me up. Have mercy!"

My room was now wrapped in intense personal sorrow. Sitting off to the side, against the wall and still on the floor, I looked and noticed a faint shaft of what appeared to be light pouring into my cell. I couldn't touch it, and wondered beyond hope what it meant. I only knew that I saw it. The accusing and mocking voices then picked up where they had left off. "Do you understand now, what you forfeited? Do you understand now, how your arrogance and rebellion has disqualified you from ever receiving anything from God? You belong to us!" they clamored. My sorrow was inconsolable. I could not stop weeping; the emotional pain was very great. The film concluded and one of the hospital staff members removed the TV from the door of my cell.

PRE-DAWN

In the days following, I was drawn again to the Bible and started reading in the Gospel of John. I noticed one change from my readings prior to Easter Sunday. As I read, the tortuous condemnation that met me previously seemed absent, yet the promise of hope was out of reach for me personally. I was constantly reminded that I was terribly lost and on the road to destruction. However, thoughts of suicide seemed to have lessened after Easter Sunday. Only one question remained: how long would this life of emptiness and sorrow last? And then what?

For the next seven months, the daily routine was fixed and predictable. I was not confined to my cell, but joined in with other patients in an array of daily recreational and educational opportunities. Although my ECT therapy treatments were concluded, I was still receiving daily medication. In the deepest part of me, I longed to know why God was ignoring my pleas. The darkness continued and I was sinking slowly into a new reality, living in twilight in a state of eternal rejection by God.

A MESSENGER SENT FROM GOD

His name was Nelson Davis. I had not seen him since my hospitalization. Nelson and I, and two other soldiers, had found each other by chance, having a common interest in Gospel music. We also learned that each of us had experience singing in quartets, which consequently resulted in the formation of our own Gospel quartet. Nelson, our top tenor was a genuine follower of Jesus. Jim, Alex and I enjoyed Gospel music but were Christians in name only, a generous assessment at best.

In a relatively short time, we had opportunities to sing in local churches. I appreciated Nelson and saw something in his spirit that was genuine. One Sunday we were invited to sing at the morning worship of a church about 100 miles from Fort Hood. After the service, one of the church members approached and invited me and the other two white members of our quartet for lunch at her home. I said, "But there are four of us in this quartet." She responded by saying that the invitation was only to the white members. Nelson, an African-American was not invited! I felt an internal anger rise and told the hostess that if all of us were not invited, then none of us would come. She apologized but held her ground. We left the church and started the long drive home.

We were getting hungry. I spotted a diner up ahead and pulled into the lot and parked right in front of the main door. Nelson was sitting in front on the passenger side, and quietly said, "Dick, I can't go in there!" I looked up to see a sign clearly stating: for "whites only." In disgust, I turned to Nelson and apologized, while inwardly being angry at the discrimination aimed at such a gentle soul as Nelson. We went straight home to Fort Hood.

It was soon thereafter that I was admitted to the hospital. Our quartet disbanded and I did not hear from any of them until after Easter. A few months went by when I was informed by hospital staff that I had a visitor. It was Nelson! In his hand was a strawberry ice cream soda and on his face, a friendly smile. Handing the soda to me he said, "Dick I've been thinking about you and praying for you. I don't know why you are here, but God wants you to know that He loves you!" Our visit lasted less than 30 minutes, but from that point on Nelson came to me weekly over the next few months with my favorite soda and the same message every time; God loved me! I waited each week for his visit and began to hope that maybe he was God's messenger with a message I desperately needed.

FROM DARKNESS TO LIGHT

One fall day, after several months of treatment, Dr. Alcott came to my cell and announced his plans for my release back to my MP unit. I was stunned. Did I hear him correctly? I didn't feel that I had made the kind of progress that would merit that news. I had to admit however that the hourly and daily assault of voices had decreased, and I hadn't had suicidal thoughts for a few months. However, I was in no way feeling confident that I could make it on my own on the outside. The doctor assured me that my future depended on my willingness to be integrated back into a normal life with my peers.

The day of my release came rather quickly. Out-processing included retrieving my military uniform and signing some papers. I was then escorted to the reception room. Looking out into the

parking lot of the hospital facility I saw a military vehicle waiting to take me back to my unit.

It was a Friday afternoon. Some of my colleagues welcomed
me back and naturally wanted to know how I was doing. I didn't
feel like talking and they seemed to understand. The next morning the barracks emptied out for weekend leisure. I had no desire
to join my fellow soldiers. I needed to take a walk and be alone.

The change of scenery outside was like walking into a world
I used to know. Being off duty, it was a welcome change to be
wearing civilian clothes once again. I wandered down a less traveled road outside the base, and in my wandering decided to walk
into a large open field. As I walked, I felt I was carrying a huge
weight of rocks, permanently fastened to me with strong shoulder straps. The rocks and their weight represented my arrogance
and rebellion and sin against God. I wondered if the ECT treatments of the previous months had accomplished anything. It
didn't seem so. Despair was a constant companion.

I decided I could no longer go on. I had no energy. I stopped
my walk. This was it! I stood motionless and cast my eyes to the
ground in a blank stare. I don't know why, but I became conscious of weeds, a few rocks and some small yellow flowers at
my feet. Focusing on one of the rocks, I thought: "Do you feel
alone rock? Do you care that no one sees or cares about you as
you spend day after day, night after night in this field?" I picked
out a weed, and asked, "Who watches over you in this field? And
who would notice you anyway? You are not worth noticing! You
have no color, nothing." Then I focused on one of the small yellow flowers. It was bright yellow, bending this way and that way
in the slight breeze over the field. I spoke to it in my mind and
said: "How can you sit there day after day and dance when no
one is watching or caring that you are even in this field?" I then

realized that "I" was looking at that flower! I, a human, was noticing! I had picked out one flower in the vast field to affirm and declare its value and acknowledge its beauty as it danced in the breeze while I watched.

I then looked heavenward into the blue sky, and in my soul cried out "Lord do you not see me in this field bent over in agony? Can you not see me as I see that flower? Do you know I am here? Why are you still silent? Am I of no value to you that you would not care about my hopelessness? Am I of no interest to you? Can you see me in this field?" I could no longer bear the weight of my rebellion and arrogance. I took one last deep breath and stood silently, motionless. Then, I sensed that someone came and stood behind me. Fear and wonder froze me in place. I did not want to turn and look, thinking I might see someone. I felt a real presence, a compassion, someone observing my bonds, noticing the weight which I could no longer carry. While trying to understand what or who it was standing behind me, I became aware that this weight on my back, representing all my sin and shame, began to shift back and forth as though someone was loosening strong straps. When the straps could no longer hold my sin and shame, my arrogance and rebellion, my sorrow and emptiness, it all fell to the ground around me. I somehow knew that all the darkness in my soul was all sinking into the soil never to be seen again. I couldn't move...I dared not move.

Unshackled, I then perceived a river of cool, crystal clear water begin to flow; first from my head, then down into my shoulders, my chest, my legs and feet. It was as though my whole body, mind, and spirit was being recreated and empowered; a light was piercing my darkness. I began to weep uncontrollably with extraordinary joy, unspeakable joy! I was overcome with joy I had never known. It was incomprehensible but I knew it was God;

He had noticed me in this open field. He had paid attention to my sorrow and had received my repentance. He sent the wind of his Holy Spirit and breathed into me new life! I knew that I had just been immersed in a freedom for which my shackled soul had fervently longed. I was now free, free in Christ! I was feeling the invigorating breeze of His embrace in that field. I had received living water from the river of life!

> *"On the last and greatest day of the festival, Jesus stood and said in a loud voice, 'Let anyone who is thirsty come to me and drink. Whoever believes in me, as Scripture has said, rivers of living water will flow from within them.' By this he meant the Spirit, whom those who believed in him were later to receive...." (John 7:37-39).*

> *"Therefore, if anyone is in Christ, the new creation has come: The old has gone, the new is here." (2 Cor. 5:17).*

With great urgency, I ran back to the barracks to retrieve my Bible. I had to read it again. A joyful hunger rose up within, and was now insatiable. Out of breath, and fumbling to open it, my eyes mysteriously fastened on 1 John 5:13 which lay on the very page to which I had randomly turned:

> *"These things I have written to you who believe in the name of the Son God, that you may know that you have eternal life" (1 John 5:13).*

My eyes stuck on the word "know." While pondering what I had just read, that gentle voice that I hadn't heard since I sat listening to that youth pastor four years earlier began to speak again. "My Son, what just happened to you in that field, is the end of your sickness. I have raised you to new life. I have heard your cries, and I have healed you! I have desired you to 'know' with certainty that I have healed your brokenness and shame, and that I have given you the gift of eternal life. What just happened out in that field is not part of your sickness; it is my gift of healing because I love you!"

Again, my joy was unspeakable and my eyes filled with grateful tears. I was simply unable to process the unlikely, unexpected, and unbelievable reality that God had not only heard my cry but loved me with profound healing. What my friend Nelson said in the hospital was true; God loved me! Nelson was the human voice expressing the divine love. I had just been rescued from the depths of despair and the shadow of death. A powerful light had penetrated my darkness. From that moment on, the Bible began to speak to me as a living document. Psalm 18 expressed the inexpressible for me:

"I love you, Lord, my strength.
The LORD is my rock, my fortress and my deliverer;
my God is my rock, in whom I take refuge,
my shield and the horn of my salvation, my stronghold.

I called to the LORD, who is worthy of praise,
and I have been saved from my enemies.
The cords of death entangled me;
the torrents of destruction overwhelmed me.
The cords of the grave coiled around me;
the snares of death confronted me.

In my distress I called to the LORD;
I cried to my God for help.
From His temple He heard my voice;
my cry came before Him, into His ears.

He reached down from on high and took hold of me;
He drew me out of deep waters.
He rescued me from my powerful enemy,
from my foes, who were too strong for me.
They confronted me in the day of my disaster,
but the LORD was my support.
He brought me out into a spacious place;
He rescued me because He delighted in me" (Ps. 18:1–6, 16–19).

SO WHO WILL BELIEVE ME, ANYONE?

Following the dramatic change in my life I discovered I had been given a gift, which later I would understand as a spiritual gift. Sharing the hope that I had found in Jesus Christ seemed to create in people a hunger for the same kind of meaning and purpose that I had found. My bunk mate, Andy, was a case in point.

One evening soon after my experience in that field, and after "lights out," I was kneeling by my footlocker in prayer. Andy, my bunkmate came in feeling his way in the semi darkness and in doing so, he tripped over me! "Herskind," he whispered, "What are you doing on your knees on the floor?" I told him I would explain in the morning.

Sure enough, the first thing on Andy's mind the next morning was the night before: "So what were you doing on the floor by your footlocker last night?" He was aware of my hospitalization, but I hadn't yet told him about the encounter that I had with God's Holy Spirit. Andy became curious and puzzled to say the least. But he listened to me as I shared as simply as I could. I told him that God so loved us that He sent Jesus to forgive us of our sin and make us His children and give to us eternal life with Him forever.

We talked some more as I tried to explain. However, I did not realize that while we were talking, Andy was about to take a thirty day leave and had to catch a train later that morning. He asked me if, when he came back from leave, we could talk some more. I agreed. Andy packed his clothes and left for vacation a few hours later.

Thirty days later, Andy returned and began talking non-stop about his vacation. "Dick, do you remember telling me that Jesus had given you a freedom which you had not known before? Well, I found it also!" I listened with amazement as he told me that when he got home, he started reading the New Testament for himself. He said Jesus opened his eyes moving him to invite Jesus into his life. I was stunned!

He continued: "Then I told my girlfriend about the new peace I had in my life, and she asked me, 'How did you discover that'?" Andy took her through some of the Scriptures he had read, and she too was moved to open her heart to Jesus! Then, on the occasion of visiting Andy's grandmother with his girlfriend, they told Grandma how Jesus had become real to them and had forgiven them of their sin. Grandma received God's gift of love in her heart! Andy seemed beside himself with joy—I was astonished!

I was amazed that my short explanation to Andy of what had happened to me resulted in a spiritual hunger in Andy which then drove him to discover from the Scriptures the answer to his own empty heart. Then, through him, his girlfriend and Grandmother receive Jesus as well. It really had little to do with me. I had just started the conversation.

A reality that has followed me as I have spoken with many others in the days and years since has revealed a similar pattern. In conversations with people, questions often turn to curiosity about the meaning of life. It is natural for me to share only what

I know - that we were created to know the grace and love of God through His son Jesus. Sharing the essence of my experience in that field where light shattered my darkness seems to open people up to consider Jesus as the possible answer to their own darkness. It is all a work of the Holy Spirit who has come to take residence in His followers. His Spirit is the gift, and I am to give human voice to those seeking meaning for their lives. I tell of many who opened their hearts to Jesus in the later chapters of this book.

SOME UNFINISHED BUSINESS

In the days and years following, I often pondered a question that I needed to have answered about this miraculous sojourn. "Why?" I asked the Lord, "why did Dr Alcott, a trained psychiatrist, working among the mentally sick and lonely, authorize a television be sent to my door on that Easter weekend? Was Dr. Alcott a believer? Was this a part of my treatment? Why else would that TV have been parked in front of my cell for that one specific hour? After all, reflecting back, it was while watching that Easter Sunday drama that the power of Jesus's death broke the power of Satan in me which led to my deep sorrow and repentance. I learned the answer to my questions many years later while visiting a pastor friend in San Francisco.

I was sharing with my friend Pastor Brian, the story of God's gracious healing in my life when I mentioned the name of the psychiatrist who cared for me, Lt. Col. Alcott of Fort Hood Texas. Pastor Brian asked, "Was his first name Benjamin?" I said yes with a large question mark etched across my face. "And he was stationed at Fort Hood?" Again I said yes. "So his name was Lt. Col. Dr. Benjamin Alcott, a psychiatrist stationed at Fort Hood, Texas?" Again I said, "Yes, but why do you ask?" Pastor Brian said, "Would you like to see him?" I choked up in disbelief and blurted out "Yes, but you are kidding right?" Pastor Brian said, "Dr Alcott is now retired and serves as a member of my congregation." I could hardly believe my ears. My friend made a phone call to the doctor, telling him that there was someone from his past who he might like to see. Soon we were on our way to visit Dr. Alcott.

I had not seen Dr. Alcott for years, but I recognized him. I extended my hand and introduced myself as one of his former patients at Fort Hood Texas in the mid-1950s. As we conversed I helped him recall how either he or one of his staff brought a TV to my cell which allowed me to watch the crucifixion of Jesus on Easter Sunday. I shared how God used that movie to show me His love as I wrestled inwardly with deep rebellion. He affirmed that he did remember me, but the details were sketchy. I then told him how God used that presentation of the death and resurrection of Jesus to bring me to a place of deep repentance in my life and set the stage for what happened after he discharged me from the hospital. I then replayed for him how God had miraculously healed me in that Texas field. I affirmed him by saying "Dr. Alcott, you were a significant part of my healing, and you have become part of my story as I have told it in small and large gatherings in the years since."

He could hardly believe that I, one of his patients of years ago, was sitting in front of him telling him of the miracle that took place after he had released me from the hospital. I thanked him for being God's caretaker on my behalf when I was in desperate need. I took pleasure in seeing the satisfaction that came to his face, knowing that God had not forgotten his role in bringing healing to this MP's life.

So, God closed the circle of that mystery and showed me that Dr. Benjamin Alcott was His servant in preparing me for the healing that God Himself was to complete. God was gracious to me and settled my curious mind by connecting me with His servant these many years later.

NOTHING SHALL BE IMPOSSIBLE

The power that was unleashed in my body in that field led me to believe that the addiction I had to cigarettes was about to meet its demise. The nicotine habit dogged me even as I read my Bible.

Early one morning, I was reading the Scripture which was now a living document to me. While reading, I had a cigarette burning. The passage that grabbed my attention was in 1 Corinthians:

> *"Do you not know that your bodies are temples of the Holy Spirit, who is in you, whom you have received from God? You are not your own; you were bought at a price. Therefore honor God with your bodies" (1 Cor. 6:19-20).*

Just then, an ash fell off my cigarette and landed right in the crease of my Bible! I calmly tilted the Bible downward while blowing the ash from the page. Then, as though Jesus was present watching this whole thing, I spoke to Him saying, "Lord, you know how I desire to make my body a temple of Your Holy Spirit. I don't want to do this anymore. But, how am I to get rid of this habit that has gripped me since I was thirteen?" I felt His Spirit answering me in my thoughts.

"The next time you light a cigarette, notice the time on the clock and write it down. Do this for one day so you have a schedule of when you typically smoke. From then on, smoke only at those times, and do so for a week. Then, increase the time between cigarettes by 10 minutes. This will start you transferring your urge to smoke originating on the inside, to the clock on the outside. By doing this faithfully for several months, and managing the time between cigarettes, you will reach a point of having only two or three cigarettes a day. Then it's only a matter of picking a day when you decide that you are free to smoke no more!"

I got excited about this strategy and faithfully carried it out for several months until I didn't need cigarettes any more. That was over six decades ago. The Lord was faithful and like a loving Father, He drew along side of me and coached me as though He was preparing me for the race for the rest of my life. Now, was it possible that I might have quit instantaneously with the Holy Spirit? I have no doubt and I am sure that for some people God has worked in that way. He surely healed me in that field in an instant of time. Perhaps I needed a lesson in discipline, and He chose this way to accomplish His purposes.

I learned many years later, the wisdom behind this method. It was explained by a psychiatrist on a TV talk show. He explained to the audience how people can stop smoking for good. The key to his strategy was a little pocket-sized computer that he had designed which the user could program to issue a beep when the time to "light up" was allowed. The timing was based on the user doing as I did at the beginning, recording how often he lit up a cigarette by writing down the time. The computer would then be programmed to increase the time between beeps to wean the user off the internal urge and smoke only on the beeps! The doctor charged a hefty price for the simple computer worn on a belt, or placed in a pocket or purse. To this day I think he owes more than a tithe on the proceeds!

While God was revealing to me how I could quit the harmful habit, I never felt any condemnation. Again, He was as a father, a coach, one who encouraged me to realize my body was the dwelling place of His Holy Spirit, not a place for me to defile. "… Everything is possible for one who believes" (Mark 9:23).

Although I was a changed person in mind and heart it was natural for the Army to move me from a military police unit to a military transportation unit. I served the remaining few months at Fort Hood, Texas and was honorably discharged.

WHERE TO, FROM HERE?

I wouldn't wish my teen years on anyone. However it was the launching pad to an adventure I could not have dreamed of or imagined. Coming home to rejoin my family was a celebration. The prodigal son had come home, and his father, mother and siblings welcomed him with open arms.

I was also pleased to be home with Joann, my high school sweetheart. We had talked about marriage after I finished my two years in the Army. However, could we now continue the planning we had done two years earlier? I knew that a conversation about the transformational changes that took place in me at Fort Hood would be challenging for me to explain and hard for her to understand. My life had been radically changed. To speak honestly about it in terms of our relationship was filled with risks, including whether or not we could go forward as a couple.

We had many discussions. I tried to explain the miracle and saw her desire to comprehend the incomprehensible and my inability to explain. In the end we reluctantly and painfully realized that it would be best to go our separate ways. I left grieving that she had waited two years for me, only to have it end in this way. Yet, something happened in the years following that showed me that God was caring for both of us.

Several years later, I received a phone call from the regional director of the Women's Christian Fellowship of Boston, asking if I would share my story at their annual banquet. This banquet was the final gathering for the current year and would be held at a hotel in the Boston area. At that time I had been married to my wife Kathy for several years, and we had two small boys.

After telling my story of the healing miracle that had taken place in my life some women came forward to the podium to express appreciation for my remarks. One of the women looked very familiar. It was Joann! I greeted her, while inwardly feeling awkward. Nevertheless I was quite surprised that she had come to the banquet. Her first words to me were "Now I understand what you were trying to tell me all those years ago." She went on to share her testimony of conversion to the person of Jesus, and the changes He had made in her life. She revealed that she was now married and had children of her own. I was so grateful to God. He had redeemed a very difficult time in our relationship and had a wonderful, though separate plan for each of us all along.

Now looking forward and realizing I had been given a new life, I asked myself what lay ahead. I could not have guessed what God had planned.

2

WALK DOWN THIS ROAD

The prophet Isaiah spoke these words to the people of Israel:

"Oh yes, people of Zion, citizens of Jerusalem, your time of tears is over. Cry for help and you'll find it's grace and more grace. The moment He hears, He'll answer. Just as the Master kept you alive during the hard times, He'll keep your teacher alive and present among you. Your teacher will be right there, local and on the job, urging you on whenever you wander left or right: 'This is the right road. Walk down this road'"... (Isa. 30:19-22 [The Message]).

With only a high school education, and a poor one at that, I now had to face the question of how God was going to guide me in getting my life started again. I was filled with motivation for whatever lay ahead, but my failure as a student in my high school days began to weigh heavily on me. God, who took me out of the darkness, was already lighting the path before me, and despite my poor academic history I was certain that He would direct me to a new and more abundant life. There was a road ahead of me. Would I, could I, walk down this road?

A conversation with my Dad opened a door for me. He had a personal friend who was the Dean at Wentworth Institute in Boston. Dad said he would talk with him and arrange an interview for me to see what the Dean might suggest. A meeting was arranged and I genuinely got excited about the possibility.

On the day of my appointment, I walked up the wide steps of Wentworth Institute dreaming of the possibility of attending there in the days to come. I stopped at the receptionist's desk and mentioned that I had an interview with Dean Swanson. She took me to his office where I was greeted as if I were a family member! As we sat together, I felt very relaxed in his presence and thanked him for meeting with me. "My Dad said it would be good for me to get your perspective on some possibilities for continuing my education. I know he has shared the events in my life of the past few years." Dean Swanson, himself a Christian, seemed eager to help.

The Dean told me that the mission of Wentworth Institute was to provide technical training for students in various vocational disciplines including associate degrees in mechanical and electrical engineering. He scheduled me for a vocational aptitude test which would reveal my interests and vocational IQ. He also had a copy of my high school academic record which I had sent prior to our meeting. Despite what he read in my records, he was optimistic that I could find a place at Wentworth, though some remedial academic work would be required to bring my academic scores to a level that would satisfy Wentworth's entrance requirements. He believed that with my motivation and an enthusiastic commitment to the challenge, I could do this remedial work within a year.

I had not heard of Newman Preparatory school, but the Dean explained that the school specialized in getting students "college ready". He then made a call on my behalf, and confirmed that Newman Prep's admissions department would meet with me that same afternoon! After preparing a letter of introduction and a copy of my high school academic records, Dr. Swanson told me I could walk from Wentworth to Newman Prep. I thanked him and left his office excited. With purpose in my steps, I started down Huntington Avenue in Boston to an important interview regarding the rest of my life!

On my way, I walked by Northeastern University, identified as such by very large letters on the middle building of three buildings. It seemed strange, but I heard again, that quiet voice in my spirit which I recognized as the Holy Spirit. "This is where you will go to school." I wondered what that meant. After all, I was on my way to a school that would qualify me for a vocational trade, not a Bachelors degree from a university. In the back of my mind was the nagging reminder that I had the handicap of a low academic record and that put Northeastern University well out of reach. I continued my walk and had my second interview of the day at Newman Prep. It was encouraging, although I began to feel a gnawing doubt about my ability to absorb the curriculum that was laid out for me. On the other hand, I was ready to go all out.

A week later, I received a letter of acceptance and welcome from Newman, and eagerly began an academic climb that would stretch me to the limits. Motivation was high however. I had an inner assurance that I was on a path that God was leading and that conviction gave me laser focus.

Being on a study regimen of eighteen hours a day, six days a week for the next nine months tested my resolve. My youngest sister holds it over me to this day, that I would not speak to her while I was studying, even shutting the door to my room while she sat outside, just wanting to sit quietly in the room with her big brother! She has since forgiven me.

I finished the grueling nine months of remedial studies, and successfully completed high school requirements in math, science, and English. I had now paid my academic debt from high school where I preferred the simpler courses offered in the business preparation track. God was clearly redeeming the time that was squandered in those four years.

As planned, I submitted an application to Wentworth Institute. However, the inner voice I heard while walking past Northeastern University earlier that year spoke again, impressing me that somehow, Northeastern University was the school I would actually attend. In pure obedience I submitted an application to the University, along with my record from Newman Prep. To my great surprise Northeastern sent me a letter of acceptance into the Bachelor of Science, Electrical Engineering degree program. My acceptance was conditioned on an acceptable performance in my first semester. I accepted the Northeastern invitation. Dr. Swanson was pleased with my choice. Indeed he had the gift of encouragement.

ME, STUDYING AT A UNIVERSITY?

My first day at Northeastern was intimidating to say the least. I felt like a fourth grader sitting in classes with people who had earned their way academically. But then, why couldn't I admit that I also had earned it as well? God had taken me this far. Lessons in trusting Him were as important as learning that handicaps were to be overcome. If this was the road to walk, I only had to start walking.

My experience at NU was a miracle of God's grace. The academic probation period came and went without incident. Beyond expectations, I was placed on the honors list in my freshman year and received an invitation into Eta Kappa Nu, an Engineering Honorary Society in my junior year.

In athletics I enjoyed playing with the Huskies, Northeastern University's football team, winning a starting position in my junior year. Judo, an enjoyable discipline from my military police training, was a sport I continued to enjoy and while at Northeastern, I founded the NU Judo Club. As a club we entered various tournaments including one at MIT across the Charles River. My spiritual life at the University was fed through weekly association with other believers in the Navigators Christian fellowship.

I knew from my experience in that field in Texas, that whatever my opportunities going forward, my life in all its expressions, would be anchored in the freedom that I had found in Jesus Christ. It was as natural as breathing for me to bring my faith to the classroom, locker room, or lunch room, even to my place of student internship. It was not out of necessity or obligation, but out of sheer gratitude that I took pleasure in sharing what God had done in my life. The guidance of the indwelling Holy Spirit was at the forefront of all my relationships and I was amazed to see the ways in which God opened spiritual conversations with my colleagues in a natural way.

One of my elective courses at Northeastern was a class on public speaking. The subject matter of each talk varied from week to week. One class assignment was to present a talk on the subject "An Important Lesson of my Life". Most students probably had to think hard about that one. On the contrary, upon hearing of the assignment I immediately knew that I would share how being of "two minds" almost destroyed my life, and how Jesus Christ filled me with purpose and direction in a secular-scientific world. The biggest challenge for me was to tell my story in seven minutes!

I presented my topic and received approval from my professor. Among his comments on my outline were the words "very interesting". After class, a fellow student asked if we could have lunch together sometime during the coming week. Andrew wanted to know how he could experience what I had found in Jesus Christ. At lunch I explained to him the Biblical message using the small New Testament I carried with me in my backpack. As we concluded our lunch, Andrew opened his heart to Jesus and right there in the busy lunch room invited Jesus into the center of his life. After telling me of the emptiness of having no meaning in his life, I understood his need and came to believe that such a need is not uncommon in the work or academic arena. Many in all walks of life are seeking meaning for their lives.

An opportunity for bringing faith to the football field was also natural for me. We were playing American International College. At this game, I played tight end on the right side of the line. There was no score. Back in the huddle I informed the quarterback that I was not being covered on some passing routes. He called a play with me in mind. The ball was snapped and I took off in the prescribed lane and caught up with a forty-seven yard pass, grabbed it, and took it into the end zone to give our team the lead, which ignited the usual end zone celebration. End zone celebrations are common in football, and my teammates entered the celebratory atmosphere. The Northeastern stands came alive with shouts and cheers, and the band got in on the action. As I was absorbing the celebration I heard that now familiar and affirming voice within tell me: "Son, look around. Remember this is the glory of men, it is fleeting and will quickly be over. My glory lasts forever." Yes, it was fleeting, and yes, it was quickly over.

Later in the locker room two of my teammates congratulated me on my first touchdown as a starting end. I responded to them with appreciation, and then shared with them what I heard in the quietness of my heart following that score; that the adulation of men is fleeting, but according to the Bible, God's glory lasts eternally. I could not help speaking for the One who pulled me up from the shadow of death into his glorious light. I didn't expect they would understand or even offer a response. In that experience I began to understand the real depth of the relationship I had with God. Opportunities to speak about the change in my life came in the most unlikely places.

THE INTERN CO-OP PROGRAM AT NORTHEASTERN

One of the unique features of the Northeastern degree program is its partnership with local industry in providing students "on the job" training in their field of study. After the freshman year the student attends a class for a six month period followed by a full time employment period of six months. Local companies interview potential students for employment in their desired field of study, to work alongside electrical engineers (in my case) learning while "doing." At graduation some students are hired and stay with the company as full time employees. Upon graduation, each student who participated in a co-op program was acknowledged to have gained two years equivalent professional experience! My "co-op" time was spent with Sylvania Electric working with engineers designing and testing aerospace electromagnetic antenna systems. This field of electrical engineering became my prime interest as I looked forward to full employment one day.

In the work environment, I was committed to giving my employer my best in time and energy in exchange for the salary and other benefits provided. I did not believe I had to put my faith on the shelf while at work. I was careful however not to use company time to have conversations with people about faith. Moreover, it was my relationship with people and the mutual respect we shared that spoke more about my faith than words. Nevertheless, conversations often took place at lunch or during coffee breaks, etc.

A study of the Gospels reveals that much of Jesus' teaching was carried out in the workplace where people sought their livelihood. He engaged tax collectors, fishermen, shepherds and members of the Roman military. It was by example that He commissioned His followers to be lights in the world. I was not ashamed of what I believed and was willing to talk about it when the opportunity would present itself. Of course, there were those who were suspicious, unable to believe that one could be genuine in their faith, especially in the secular workplace. Some were willing to test that conviction as I learned one day.

I was enjoying a sandwich at lunch when a group of my colleagues gathered about thirty feet from my desk to discuss the Red Sox game the night before. As an avid Red Sox fan myself, I decided to chime in on the conversation. As the discussion progressed, Barry joined the circle. He interrupted the conversation declaring that he had a hilarious story and wanted to share it. We all turned to listen. As the "joke" progressed, I could see where it was going and determined it was not the kind of story I wanted to affirm. I turned quietly and feeling vulnerable, left the circle to go back to my desk. I sensed that a few eyes were following me, wondering what was going on. It wasn't long before laughter broke out, the group disbanded and returned to work.

Later that afternoon, a colleague who was in that circle stopped by my desk and said, "Dick, you did the right thing by leaving our discussion circle at lunch today." I said, "Oh, how so, what do you mean?" "Well, Barry came into the circle for a purpose. He had been sent by a few of our colleagues to tell that story while they watched from a distance, just to see how you would respond!" Evidently, some in my circle of work relationships wished to know if my faith was more than talk. Perhaps it was their purpose to expose hypocrisy in those who claim faith, or maybe it was a testing on their part to see if my faith was real enough to provide potential meaning for their lives. Whatever the case, I learned that a follower of Jesus can expect that one's faith might be tested. So it was for me that day.

Having conversations with co-workers about faith confirmed a conviction that all people are alike; wanting the same things in life—peace, joy, and love. They are hard working, many supporting families and all facing challenges in the workplace, community and at home. Life without faith had been horrific for me. Some of my co-workers, no doubt, were seeking answers for their own struggles and challenges. The results of many such conversations are known only to God.

NEW DESTINATIONS

Graduation time at Northeastern University was approaching, as was the conclusion of my work as a student engineer at Sylvania. I was now at a new crossroads. My department manager at Sylvania engaged me in a conversation about my future. I told him that I had been thinking about graduate school, and he told me in turn, that he wished to make me an offer for continued employment following graduation! I expressed my appreciation for the offer, but reiterated my desire for graduate study. He then strongly suggested the University of Illinois as offering one of the best Electromagnetic Engineering programs in the country. He told me that if graduate study was important to me, then the

University of Illinois would be a good investment. He even offered to provide a recommendation for my application.

I appreciated and respected his perspective. I also knew that by taking his advice, I would be stepping up to another academic level. Strangely, despite my success at Northeastern, the possibility of continuing study at the University of Illinois awakened the memory of academic inferiority that had taken me to Newman Prep several years earlier. Why it continued to surface now and then, I don't know. But it always turned me back to God for a deeper lesson in trust; that I might always remember that my life was not my own and that I was bought with a price (1 Cor. 7:23). Furthermore, I firmly believed that God was leading my life, even placing people in my life who had credentials to evaluate my potential. If God was in this then why would I not follow the opportunity and exchange my lack of self-confidence for an increase in faith in the One who gave me this new life?

In the end, I sent an application to both schools: Northeastern University's graduate program and the graduate program at the University of Illinois in Champaign-Urbana, Illinois. To my surprise I was accepted at both schools! I decided to study at the University of Illinois and was persuaded that this was "the way" and I was to "walk in it!"

THE FIGHTIN' ILLINI

In the fall of 1962 I headed west in my little green Volkswagen and made arrangements to stop and visit a lovely lady whom I had met a week earlier at a national gathering of college students in Boca Raton, Florida. The quadrennial gathering provided opportunity for college students from across the US to gather for a week of inspiration and Christian fellowship.

I knew nothing about Jamestown, New York but became very interested in the young lady who lived there. In fact, that visit kindled a long distance relationship that had a purpose far beyond a stop over in Jamestown, NY. There is more on that later.

While driving onto the campus of the university I could tell that football was in the air. This was Big Ten country and the home of the "Fightin' Illini." After getting acquainted with the campus, finding my dorm, visiting the bookstore, and getting settled in general, I was ready to begin graduate studies in electrical engineering.

Again my nemesis (that deep sense of academic inadequacy) raised its head in the very first semester of the two year graduate program. After completing the first semester courses and exams, I received a warning notice from the university; my grades indicated substandard performance for a graduate program. Though passing the courses, I was placed on probation and was allowed to continue my studies pending improvements in the next semester. A period of discouragement set in as I prepared for the second semester. Should I have settled for Northeastern University which I knew? Did my department manager at Sylvania not understand my limits? Did I hear God correctly?

I rehearsed the unbelievable journey of the past few years, which now included success at Northeastern and at Sylvania, and chose to believe that God's love and direction had not failed despite the notice from the University. Scripture once again provided what I needed to hear.

> *"Trust in the Lord with all your heart and do not lean unto your own understanding. In all your ways acknowledge him, and he shall direct your paths" (Prov. 3:5-6).*

Resisting discouragement, I reaffirmed my trust in Him. If He gave me the gifts adequate for the task He called me to do, I would trust Him with the intellectual capacities He had also given me and complete what I had come to do. I chose to believe that being at Illinois was not a mistake. I chose to follow.

In the second semester, I felt empowered with faith and focused on going forward. I repeated the academic experience at Northeastern and was subsequently inducted into Alpha Chapter of the Chi Gamma Iota Veteran's Scholastic Honor Society in October of 1963. I squeezed every point I could out of my studies including an exam which I took on the last day of finals my second and final year. Finally finished, I was driving the interstate heading for Jamestown, NY when I realized I had not shown an important step in my analysis of an examination question. I stopped off the Interstate, found a phone booth and dialed my professor long distance (no cell phones back then). Fortunately he was in his office.

"Professor, I am calling to clarify something on my final exam." I then explained that I left out a step in the analysis of one of the exam questions. I am sure he had never received a long distance call from a student who wished to make a correction on his final exam from a telephone booth at a rest stop. As I explained, he told me that I was correct, although I never knew if he allowed it to count. Nevertheless, I rested and learned later that I had passed the exam with room to spare.

While the academic challenge at Illinois was my main concern, my Judo interests were still active. As at Northeastern University earlier, I found some students at the University of Illinois with similar interests. Receiving permission from the University Student Activities department, a University Judo Club was formed. The club grew to approximately thirty-five "judokas." A black belt, Rett Somerville, became our black belt authority in residence. He had the authority to promote Judokas to various degrees of Judo expertise and was instrumental promoting me to a NIKYU, a second degree brown belt. Soon we discovered that Purdue University had a Judo club and worked with them to create a Big Ten intercollegiate match at the University of Illinois. I believe Purdue won the match. However, our Judo club took great pleasure in introducing Judo into intercollegiate competition.

AN ECLIPSE, CLOSE UP AND PERSONAL

My studies at Illinois included a project sponsored by the US Government. The project included the development of a large, very low frequency antenna placed in the open spaces of the farmlands of Illinois. The purpose of the antenna was to allow measurement of the changes in the ionosphere during and after a lunar eclipse. It was a clever use of natural phenomena in which the moon was used as a "switch" to shut the sun off and on again during the test. The scientific interest was associated with the behavior of electrons in the atmosphere during the "on-off" time period, and how the electrons changed the composition of the ionosphere. While the project was interesting, getting to and from the site over several weeks was more fun involving a small university airplane for our transportation.

We traveled to the site daily in a Piper Cub, a two-seated training aircraft owned by the university's flight school. Project Manager Bob was a PHD student and the pilot, and I was his graduate assistant. The test site was about 100 miles from the university. Bob had received his advanced pilot license from the school. The plane we flew in was equipped with dual controls. A pilot instructor could, therefore, release control of the aircraft to the student in a flight training session.

I have vivid memories of that first flight.

On our first day of travel, we arrived at the University Illini Airfield, located our plane, and started pre-flight checks of the aircraft. The plane seemed awfully snug to me. I circled the plane, touching the wings and fuselage. It was all canvas! I could actually push on the canvas and move it about a quarter of an inch! It just seemed flimsy, but I didn't complain since everything seemed normal to Bob.

With pre-flight checks completed we both boarded the plane through the flimsy door on each side, and squeezed into rather small seats. I was thankful that I did not have claustrophobia, though I thought I might come down with it shortly. Both seats had the same controls including pedals for the feet and a yoke for the hands, and a clear view of the instrument panel.

All set to go, we taxied out to the runway and in a few moments were airborne. About thirty minutes into the flight Bob said, "Would you like to do some maneuvers?" I responded by saying, "I guess so. What do you have in mind?" Bob explained that he would first do a 'stall' maneuver, that would put us into a spin.

"Really," I said. "Well, ok, I assume you've done this before." He assured me that it was safe. Before I knew it we were in a fall, spinning with the nose pointing directly at the cornfields below. Looking down, I began to feel dizzy as the corn stalks were definitely getting bigger by the second. My stomach started objecting. I assumed that Bob was experiencing the same and that concerned me. He glanced over at me and saw that I was struggling turning pale. He pulled out of the spin and returned to normal flight. Then noticing my ashen face, Bob said "Well,

I guess we won't do any more of those today. Are you OK?" I managed to say, "I think so". Frankly I was ready to heave! I was happy to provide a little sport for him and thanked him for not doing any more of those "stalls into spins" deals. He certainly was competent and unaffected by the whole event.

About twenty minutes later, he asked if I would like to fly the plane. I said "Okay". I had always wanted to fly a plane and here was my chance. "So what do I do?" I asked. He responded "You are an engineer, figure it out!" I had controls on my side of the plane and he showed me the function of each lever and pedal and what each did. Although I actually flew the plane, he had absolute control if I did anything foolish, like trying one of his spins!

After practicing a few minutes I asked, "So, how do we get where we are going?" Bob replied, "Well, you can set the compass or you can follow the highway right below you." So I flew the plane for about twenty minutes following the highway below, and then willingly gave control back to Bob. I was now ready for a movie and a pillow for my head!

Approaching our destination, we spotted the windsock located on a small building at the side of the landing strip of grass. Bob checked the direction of the windsock in order to choose which end of the airstrip we would use for our approach. We started our descent and in a few minutes our wheels touched down. However our landing speed was quite fast and we continued to roll toward a small hill at the end of the runway. Our momentum carried us half way up the hill! When the plane stopped, it fishtailed backwards until we were back on the end of the runway.

Bob admitted, with embarrassment, that he had misread the windsock and landed with the wind to our back rather than into a headwind, giving us too much speed while landing. Some farmers watched the whole thing and tried to hide their laughter. Now that we were safe on the ground, I could say that it was all fun getting to the antenna site. We flew to our site several times as we made final preparations for the lunar eclipse in order to provide the means for collecting the data we were seeking. Since then, I prefer flying commercial airlines. They don't do spins over cornfields and do provide snacks and movies along the way. I can't recall ever flying in a Piper Cub after that project was completed.

THE CONTINUING INTEREST IN JAMESTOWN

Interest in the connection between Jamestown and Champagne-Urbana Illinois grew dramatically while I studied at the university. There were several weekends when I took my green Volkswagen and made my way to New York. Kathy and I both believed that our meeting in Boca Raton a year earlier was not by chance and that God was behind the scenes bringing us together.

We first met, almost by chance, near the end of a conference for Christian college students. Our first meeting occurred when a buddy and I were walking the beach. We noticed two young ladies taking a final swim about thirty yards off shore and agreed that we should go and "investigate" them. We edged our way into their conversation, when I noticed that one of them was very cute ~ no, she was beautiful! She had a slight scar on her cheek and for some reason it endeared me to her. I managed to invite her to take a walk along the beach, and left my buddy talking. As we walked, I wondered how we could continue this relationship when we had only hours before packing up and returning to our homes, separated by many miles.

Learning that she was from Jamestown, NY, I put a map in my mind and realized that one week later I would be passing Jamestown on my to the University of Illinois. With my fingers crossed, I got the courage to ask her if I could stop by and see her on my way to school. She agreed and arranged for me to stay at her parents' house for a few days. Our first evening together was not what I had in mind. She had to work and asked me if I would take her place at a meeting at the church where she was supposed to give a report on the conference. I was disappointed to say the least. Here was another block in the road to getting to know this pearl I had found on a Florida beach. I did not know where the church was and knew no one from that church, yet there I was at the debriefing. I can't remember a thing I said, as I was only thinking of her! The next day we spent time sharing our lives, and reflecting on the retreat at Boca Raton. That evening, I took her to a war movie, the only movie in town.

The door that truly opened us to each other was our faith. We shared how we each came to know Jesus. She told me how her struggle with life almost ended at her own hands with an overdose of aspirin. After God stepped in and saved her from harming herself, He intervened and provided a mature Godly woman who led Kathy into a deep relationship with Jesus. Our common faith has been our bond for over fifty years. She has been a wonderful gift from God.

One weekend I invited her to come to the university. I bought tickets to our homecoming game with Michigan State University. Neither of us remember who won the game. We just remember the school spirit of a Big Ten game with the "Fightin' Illini" and the joy of being together for a weekend.

After the game we went out to dinner and with a strong case of jitters, I asked her if she would marry me! She said she "would have to pray about it." Yikes! The next morning we went to church together and afterward she said "yes." Later she called her parents in Jamestown and announced to them that she was getting married! They responded by asking, "To who?"

It was frustrating being separated by such distance, communicating by letters and phone calls. I wanted to complete my offer of marriage by giving her an engagement ring. Thanksgiving was coming up and I started shopping for the ring which I would take home at Thanksgiving break. I had planned to take her out to a nice restaurant for dinner and give the ring to her between the meal and dessert. However, the ring was burning a hole in my pocket and at lunch that day, over a bologna sandwich, I pulled it out and reaffirmed my desire for her to be my wife. I put the ring on her finger and told her that I loved her. The rest is a fifty-two year history with two sons and nine grandchildren.

Our race to the altar had begun, but another race already in progress was capturing world attention. Little did I know that I would find myself running in that race as well, a race literally out of this world. Training for that would continue in days ahead.

3

THE RACE TO SPACE

On October 4, 1957, the world was told to look up and view man's first satellite orbiting the earth. The Soviet Union had started the space race. I recall looking skyward as the sun was setting and spotting Sputnik, man's first successful orbit of a spherical ball, gliding silently across the evening sky. With lots of curiosity but never a thought that I would one day have a part in that great task of space and planetary exploration, I simply wondered.

Seven years later, in the spring of 1964 with a resume in progress and a graduate degree pending, the prospects of working in the aerospace industry had become real and exciting. The trip from Dean Swanson's office at Wentworth Institute, to the present moment at the University of Illinois was beyond my expectations. I was full of hope and thanking God for his faithfulness. Life was full of excitement and still unfolding before me.

One of the aerospace research facilities hiring graduate electrical engineers was NASA's Jet Propulsion Laboratory located at the base of the San Gabriel mountain range in Pasadena, California. Managed by the California Institute of Technology, JPL is at the forefront of interplanetary spacecraft design and development. It seemed unreal that I was boarding a plane bound for Los Angeles to interview at JPL and meet people I might be working with in the near future. The employment interview and tour of JPL gave my dreams more substance. I continued in hope, knowing that the God who brought me from the shadow of death and into His light had plans for my whole life. Whether or not this phase of my life would be at JPL, I would trust Him either way. JPL was not the only opportunity available. Several other companies had also expressed interest.

A few weeks after the JPL interview, I received an envelope with a JPL return address. I opened it with heart pumping and read an invitation to join the Spacecraft Antenna section, as an Antenna Research Engineer. I called Kathy to give her the great news that I had received an offer to work at JPL! I sent my acceptance letter on May 8, 1964, asked for and received a start date of July 13th. That approval allowed Kathy and I to fulfill our plan to be married in New York on June 27th.

A CEREMONY IN JAMESTOWN AND A CROSS COUNTRY HONEYMOON

To attend the University of Illinois' graduation ceremonies for an advanced degree would have been wonderful after all the hard work of study, but I couldn't be in two places at once. I had a more important ceremony to attend in Jamestown, New York - our wedding!

Our courtship was not the normal kind, since we were separated by many miles. We joked at the end of the first two weeks of marriage that those two weeks represented the longest time we had ever spent together! It didn't matter since we shared the conviction that God had brought us together, and whatever lay ahead, He was the bond that would keep us together. To write this many years later is a humbling confirmation of our common faith and God's faithfulness to His promises.

We were married in Kathy's home church, the First Covenant Church of Jamestown. While planning the wedding ceremony, she asked me if I would sing "The Wedding Prayer", a song which described our desire for God's blessing through the coming years. I told her I would. I then told my Dad I had committed to sing that song to Kathy during the ceremony. He gently and wisely warned me that if I did, I should not look at her while singing. He said, "Pick a spot on the wall just over her shoulder so as to not let the emotions of the moment affect your voice." Wise instruction as it turned out! With a congregation of family and friends in the pews, the wedding party in place, and the ceremony in progress, the time came for me to sing.

Our Weddding in Jamestown

I picked a spot on the wall just over Kathy's shoulder and started to sing. All was going well, so well that I took my eyes off the wall and focused on her smiling face. Bad idea! As my eyes caught hers, my voice started to quiver. I was about to lose my place in the song, and quickly refocused on the wall, recovering before too much damage had been done! Later, no guest commented "what happened when…" so I guess it was not that noticeable, except to me and Kathy. Every anniversary since, we have played the tape of our wedding and at the right time, we will often say "there it is" referring to my struggle to maintain composure.

Our honeymoon was a cross country tour of interesting places. One place on my list was Champaign, Illinois where I had befriended a local news TV broadcaster while attending the U of I. I wanted Kathy to meet him. The meeting wasn't to be face to face, but TV to face. We did not have a hotel reservation, but hoped there would be a room available with a TV. With the telecast only minutes away, we rushed into the lobby and told the registrar we needed a room. He looked at us with a question mark written on his face and proceeded to peruse his room schedule. A room was available. Following registration we rushed to the room and watched the evening local news delivered by my friend. Only later did we realize with great laughter what the registrar might have been thinking about these newlyweds and their urgent need for a room!

The next major stop was Loveland, Colorado where my uncle was a pastor in the Evangelical Covenant Church of America. In the summer, he ran a youth camp in the Rocky Mountains. Knowing we were coming west, he offered his home in Loveland for a honeymoon destination. Loveland was a quaint town full of red hearts hanging on each lamppost. Kathy and I had the first fight of our marriage when high in the Rockies in July we had a snowball fight! Her throws were amazingly accurate.

The Grand Canyon of Arizona was a spectacular site. We learned that you can take a donkey ride down into the canyon. I was disappointed to have them tell me that I was a few pounds over the maximum allowed weight and would not be allowed to ride the donkey.

Just before sunrise the next day we headed west and arrived in Pasadena, California before the sun went down. Our Volkswagen Karman Gia, served us well on our travels from Jamestown. In the small trunk under the hood were some of our clothes and a few pots and pans. The car also carried a big dream for both of us; married, working and loving it.

Before checking into our California hotel, we found the Pasadena Covenant Church which was affiliated with our denomination. We arrived just before office closing time, and told an administrative assistant that we had just arrived from the East Coast and, as a newly married couple, would like to meet some young married couples in the days to come. To our great surprise, we learned that the young married couples group was having a pool party that very evening and that we would surely be welcome there. With address in hand, we found the party and immediately felt we had hit a jackpot of potential young married friendships.

Now, only one weekend away, my dream job was foremost on my mind. I was ready for Monday my first day at JPL, to start my dream job with NASA and the space program.

4

A DREAM JOB

Temporary accommodations in Pasadena were provided for us as we searched for rental housing. Monday, I would make my first entrance to the parking lot at JPL. I was excited to be there and felt humbled that God would provide this opportunity to participate in the exploration of space.

JPL Entrance Gate

Upon arriving at the facility nestled against the foothills of the San Gabriel mountain range, I located the administration building and introduced myself at the main desk as a new employee reporting to the Spacecraft Antenna Systems group. The chief engineer of the Space Antenna Systems group met me in the lobby and welcomed me to JPL. We went to his office where he briefed me on the activities currently active in the Spacecraft Antenna systems group and showed me to my office.

It didn't take long to get familiarized with my new surroundings and I soon learned that I would be doing some research in advanced spacecraft antenna applications. I was also informed that I would be assigned to the flight support team for the upcoming Surveyor 1 flight to the moon. Surveyor was a series of seven unmanned spacecrafts designed to test the moon's surface, and retrieve information about the nature of the lunar surface in support of the Apollo mission, a program for sending a man to the moon.

My responsibilities in support of Surveyor 1 included technical support for the communication antennas which facilitate sending commands and data to and from the spacecraft. To become familiar with the spacecraft necessitated an up close and personal visit which required a trip to the manufacturer, Hughes Aircraft in Culver City.

AN INTRODUCTION TO "ITS MAJESTY"

The fifteen minute JPL helicopter flight across the Los Angeles basin to Hughes Aircraft Company took us across the city during rush hour. It was a strange site seeing the smog of those days hovering above the interstate highway system. Smog was a serious problem in Los Angeles in the mid sixties, and the automobile was a major source of the pollution.

After exiting the helipad at Hughes, we were led to the "cleanroom" area where Surveyor 1 was going through its assembly and testing prior to its shipment to Cape Canaveral. Before entering the "clean room", we covered our street clothes with white smocks, gloves and head coverings which gave us the momentary illusion of being part of a emergency hospital medical staff. The main spacecraft assembly and test area projected an aura of being germ free. There in the middle of the room, mounted on a raised pedestal was the ten foot tall - fourteen foot wide *Surveyor 1 Lunar Spacecraft*. It was dressed in polished aluminum surfaces giving it a regal authority, demanding respect from those in its presence. Soon this robotic craft would be in transit to the surface of the moon some 235,000 miles from earth.

Surveyor was an ingenious creation sharing some of the physical characteristics of its human creators. It had arms, legs, a head, ears, and body.

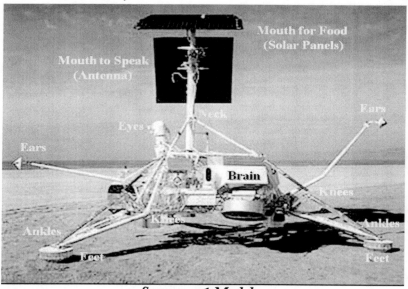

**Mouth for Food
(Solar Panels)**

**Mouth to Speak
(Antenna)**

Neck

Ears

Eyes

Ears

Brain

Knees

Knees

Ankles

Ankles

Feet

Feet

Surveyor 1 Model
(Labels by Author)

The thought occurred to me that we had created a "man" in our own image. The image analogy was intriguing. Surveyor's head included a solar panel designed to feed off the sun's energy, converting it into electrical currents to provide the "life blood" flowing within its body. Also on its head was a large panel antenna which provided for transmission of electronic speech (photos and data) back to earth. Surveyor's "brain" was located in a highly polished aluminum container which enclosed the communications and command electronics.

During the mission, all information and commands, to and from the spacecraft, would pass through this brain. A television camera mounted on one side of this mechanical man represented its eyes. Surveyor's legs were of brilliant design as well. During landing, the craft would fall freely while absorbing a mild landing shock through hydraulically designed "knee"and "ankle" joints attached to "foot pads".

Later models of Surveyor had a mechanical hand in the form of a telescoping bucket designed to collect lunar soil. Small Omni-directional antennas located at the end of booms stuck far out to the sides simulating Surveyor's "ears". These ears were designed to receive and transmit data during flight, providing all two-way communications. The electronic "ears" were of particular interest to me. If there were technical problems involving those "ears" during lunar transit or landing, my team and I would provide support to space flight operations in

A Selfie on the Moon

helping to solve those problems. There was something magical about being twelve inches from the very antennas for which I would provide flight support. Before leaving the clean room I whispered, "Bon voyage!"

One of the first pictures sent back to earth from Surveyor 1 was a picture of the spacecraft's own shadow on the surface of the moon. Like any traveler to a new destination, taking a "selfie" seemed appropriate!

SOBER REFLECTIONS

Surveyor's body was truly an engineering marvel. I could not help drawing upon my familiarity with the Bible, and noticing a comparison with the record of the creation of mankind in the image of God. The image in Genesis was of course, not an image of the physical nature, but the image of spirit with mind, will, and emotions. With all due respect for the extraordinary intelligence that had gone into Surveyor's design and development, it occurred to me that we had created a man in our own image, after our own likeness, and as we viewed what we had created we declared it very good (Gen. 1:30).

The helicopter back to JPL allowed me additional time for reflection on the mechanical man I had just seen. Realizing that this robot was the product of intelligent minds, and designers of extraordinary ability, it seemed strange that despite the ingenious creativity of mankind, many see themselves as simply a biological evolution in a vast impersonal universe. It increased my conviction that we ourselves are, as the Scriptures declare, made in the image of God, in his likeness (Gen. 1: 26).

PREPARATIONS FOR LAUNCH

Over the next several months my work, along with a team of technicians, was focused on ensuring that the antenna test facility on the mesa was ready for any emergency requiring test data to support the functioning of the on-board omni-antenna system. Fabrication and testing of an accurate model of the spacecraft was crucial toward this end.

This effort allowed us to simulate any problems, including antennas not deploying after launch. A deployment failure did in fact occur on Surveyor 1 and will be discussed later.

Surveyor Antenna Test Model

GOD IN THE MIX

Several days prior to the launch of Surveyor 1 from Cape Kennedy, I was working long hours, including a few times until the wee hours of the morning. On one occasion past midnight, I took a break to get a cup of coffee. While walking to the coffee room, I thought of an article I had been reading in Time Magazine with the cover title "IS GOD DEAD?" With that in mind, and a cup of coffee in hand, I turned to go back to my desk when a maintenance employee came out of a nearby office. I said hello to him, and quite spontaneously said "Did you see the latest issue of Time magazine?" He answered "No." I continued, "Some theologians seem to be suggesting that perhaps God is dead. What do you think, is God dead?"

His interest in my question seemed genuine, and began a conversation in which we discussed how we can know if God exists, and if He does, can we know Him personally. As we talked I sensed through the Holy Spirit that this maintenance person had some past exposure to the Christian faith but did not seem to understand the implications of Jesus' life, death and resurrection. After explaining to him more fully, I showed him from Scripture that by trusting what God says concerning Jesus, we can experience the reality of God in a tangible though mysterious way. I explained that faith connects us with God who changes our identity in this world, forgives our sin, and gives us freedom and purpose in our lives. I shared briefly how I found life through faith in Jesus a few years earlier. I told him that he could enter into a personal relationship with God through Jesus Christ. I sensed that the Holy Spirit was present in our conversation, so I asked the young man if he wished to enter into that relationship with Jesus as well. He surprised me with a quick "yes"! We prayed together by that coffee machine as he confessed his sin, and received Jesus, God's gift to him.

Just as we were concluding our conversation another maintenance employee appeared. Thinking he might have heard our conversation I said to him, "Hi, did you hear what we were talking about?" He replied, "Yes, I was listening from the other room!" I thought, "Wow, this can't be!" As we talked, it was clear that he also desired to find meaning for his life, and he received Jesus in that early morning hour. I spent a little more time with them, encouraging them to spend some time studying the Gospels daily, to strengthen their relationship as followers of Jesus. I went back to my desk, energized and motivated by the fact that much of Jesus' own ministry was in the workplace. Why not at work, in the wee hours of the morning, while taking a coffee break on the way to the moon!

In subsequent days I began to wonder if there were others at JPL with an interest in what the Bible has to say about life and our purpose for being here. I spoke to a few of my colleagues who I believed were open to a Bible study. And so we began to meet once a week with a brown bag lunch. Over the years, I found that people in the workplace are hungry for meaning that goes far beyond coming to work every day. One engineer, with whom I became a friend as well as a colleague, had his own encounter with Jesus, but more on that later.

After many months the time had come. Liftoff to the moon was scheduled for a holiday in May, a Memorial day weekend that would remain etched in my memory these many years later.

5

DESTINATION MOON

On Memorial Day weekend, May 30 of 1966, I was listening on the radio to the play by play at liftoff. I became concerned when the news coverage indicated that shortly after liftoff, one of the omni-antennas may have failed to deploy as planned. My phone rang and with haste I rushed to the lab.

On the mesa located above and behind the JPL complex, we hoisted the full scale model spacecraft on a mount with antennas positioned to simulate the conditions that were thought to exist on the spacecraft as it raced to the moon. The flight data indicated that one of the two omni-antennas was still folded against the "mast" (neck)

Antenna Test Range

of the spacecraft and had not deployed during launch. In essence the two antennas could be interfering with one another causing

79

"communication holes" between earth and the spacecraft. If such conditions existed, there was the potential problem of losing control of Surveyor at crucial times during the flight or landing sequence. My support team and I simulated the conditions on the spacecraft, and recorded the data on magnetic tape so that Space Flight Operations could assess whether the midcourse correction and landing sequence would be jeopardized.

I recall taking the data to Space Flight Operations, knowing that a whole mission could be depending on what our data revealed. I felt "just a little pressure" as I gave the test data to the Space Flight Operations engineers. We had checked and double checked to make sure we had captured the conditions occurring on the spacecraft.

As it turned out, the antenna deployment problem did not affect the mid-course correction maneuvers. However preparation for landing, included reorienting the spacecraft to avoid potential problems caused by the one partially deployed omni-antenna.

A surprise was discovered upon landing. The spacecraft signaled that a full deployment of the partially deployed antenna had occurred at the moment of touchdown. The antenna was deployed either by the vibrations of the landing rockets, or the mild jolt of landing on the surface. Information started streaming to earth providing photographs and scientific data. Our "image man" was safely on the moon and could start its historic mission, collecting information that would allow representatives of mankind to step on the moon one day.

FLASH BACK

After the astonishing success of Surveyor 1, my mind flashed back to the moment when I was first introduced to Surveyor by way of a technical document describing the mission itself. As

I read, it occurred to me that I was engaged in the reading of a parable, a means of conveying a truth by way of a story that helps the mind understand. Jesus taught truths by telling stories from the world of experience. His stories are in the form of the parables found in the Gospels.

While reading the flight plan for Surveyor, a most compelling parable came to mind. Just as the actual spacecraft was designed to land on the moon, so we, made in the image of God were also created with a destination in mind. For mankind, that destination is an eternal relationship with God.

To accomplish a safe and productive journey, Surveyor was equipped to communicate with its human creator during flight. If Surveyor strayed off course, in danger of missing the mark, the flight engineers at NASA had the ability to send information and instructions to the spacecraft which, if received and enacted upon, would result in a mid-course correction allowing the spacecraft to be re-directed towards its planned destination—a safe landing.

A MID-COURSE CORRECTION FOR MANKIND

As I was reading the flight plan for Surveyor, it occurred to me that the mid-course correction idea was not new to the space age. It originated not with aerospace engineers, but with God. Mankind was created to have eternal fellowship with God, but as history demonstrates, the journey of all mankind has run off course relative to God's intentions. The Scripture declares:

> *"As it is written: "There is no one righteous, not even one; there is no one who understands; there is no one who seeks God. All have turned away, they have together be-*

come worthless; there is no one who does good, not even one" (*Rom. 3:10-12*).

The human family is in need of a personal mid-course correction while journeying through this life. Like Surveyor, we need information from "home", to inform us how to get back on track to eternal fellowship with our Creator. The source of that information is the Bible.

The great difference in our journey through life compared to Surveyor's journey is that we live in more than a three-dimensional space. We also live in a moral and spiritual space in which God has given us the gift of choice. The moral and spiritual choices we make carry consequences. Our choices can bring joy, meaning, purpose to life, and service to others, or darkness, lack of direction, interpersonal frustration and self-absorption. Any observer of the human condition knows that the human race is off-course; that there are counter forces that lead the whole world astray (Rev. 12:9).

The Bible states that we all have responded alike in this spiritual and moral universe. The people of all nations have chosen a path which is self-centered and as a result, our "hearing" has become dull (Matt. 13:15-16). Created for a destiny of enjoying a personal and intimate relationship with our creator, we find ourselves without bearing, having no knowledge of why we are here nor where we are going. In the end, our self-centered orientation leads to spiritual decay and death. "For the wages of sin is death" (Rom. 6:23). The death referred to is not simply the state of cessation of physical life, though it is that, but also a condition called spiritual death, an eternal separation from our Creator, in whose image we are made. We have a sense of being off course from our purpose by an inner restlessness, confusion and a wandering through life with a lack of purpose. We live in a state of spiritual blindness, regret, sorrow, agony of spirit and hopelessness of heart.

But there is a mid-course correction for all created in the image of God. In the moral realm as in the physical, God does not change His laws to fit the situation. He works within the law to produce the outcome He desires. Death continues to be the consequence for violation of the spiritual law. God, however, uses death and the spiritual law to effect a change for us, similar to the way that the engineer uses the laws of celestial mechanics to implement the mid-course correction for a robotic space vehicle. A spiritual mid-course correction results in a re-orientation toward God and His purposes. To bring about that re-orientation, we, like Surveyor, have to be informed with mid-course correction information.

THE MID-COURSE CORRECTION INFORMATION

God's mid-course correction plan is communicated to us in the person of Jesus Christ. The Bible says that Jesus "became sin for us that we might become the righteousness of God" (2 Cor. 5:21). His life, death and resurrection proclaims that while we were still in our sin (being off course), Christ died for us, so that in a spiritual exchange, men off-course could be redirected to fellowship with God. The Old Testament foreshadows God's plan for mankind and the New Testament reveals that plan in the coming of Jesus Christ. Consider for a moment the foreshadowing from the Old Testament.

God chose the nation of Israel as the means of communicating His love, mercy and grace to a broken world. It was not on the basis of perfection that Israel was chosen to demonstrate the path to spiritual redirection. It was solely God's disposition of love for Israel.

> *"But it was because the Lord loved you and kept the oath he swore to your ancestors that he brought you out with a mighty hand and redeemed you from the land of slavery, from the power of Pharaoh king of Egypt" (Deut. 7:8).*

For four centuries, Israel had suffered under a heavy and unspeakably cruel enslavement in Egypt. In their misery, the people of Israel pleaded with God for relief. He heard their cry and revealed a plan to set them free. God revealed that He was going to send destruction to every first born of Egyptian families and spare Israel's families and lead them to freedom. The instructions to Israel were clear, though mysterious.

On the day designated for freedom, the families of Israel were to prepare a meal involving a lamb from the flocks. They were to take the blood of a lamb and wipe it over the door frame of their homes. The destroyer, when seeing the blood over the door of the families of Israel, would "passover" those homes, sparing the household.

> *"The blood will be a sign for you on the houses where you are, and when I see the blood, I will pass over you. No destructive plague will touch you when I strike Egypt"*
> *(Ex. 12:13).*

In receiving and acting upon that plan, a mid-course correction became effective for the enslaved. The destroyer passed over the households of the Israelites, who were then set free. God dwelt among the people of Israel, leading them out of slavery to freedom in a land promised to them.

THE NEW TESTAMENT FULFILLMENT

The Old Testament ritual of a blood sacrifice of Passover lambs finds its ultimate expression in the Easter event.

> *"In the past God spoke to our ancestors through the prophets at many times and in various ways, but in these last days he has spoken to us by his Son, whom he appointed heir of all things, and through whom also he made the universe" (Heb. 1:1-2).*

The apostle John introduced Jesus of Nazareth as "the Lamb of God who takes away the sins of the world" (John 1:29). The blood of the lamb which set ancient Israel free from its bondage to a crushing dictator, points to the blood spilled in the death of Jesus Christ, by crucifixion.

As Israel came under the blood of that Passover lamb, so all who place themselves under the covering of Jesus' blood are spared destruction, and set back on course to their original destination, which is eternal fellowship with God who loves them.

> *"But God raised him from the dead, freeing him from the agony of death, because it was impossible for death to keep its hold on him" (Acts 2:24).*

> *"Yet to all who did receive him, to those who believed in his name, he gave the right to become children of God—"* *(John 1:12).*

A mid-course correction in life is found in the cross of Jesus Christ through personal faith in the power of His blood to cover sins. Jesus' sinless life, death, and resurrection is the witness to His authority over death and life. Through the resurrection God gave a sign to mankind -- that the spiritual "off-course" condition has been corrected so that those with faith can be assured of a new course for life. God is no respecter of persons; those in any nation upon the earth are covered where faith in Jesus Christ is found.

> *"Listen! I stand at the door and knock. If anyone hears My voice and opens the door, I will come in to him and have dinner with him, and he with Me" (Rev. 3:20 [HCSB]).*

> *"Therefore, if anyone is in Christ, the new creation has come: The old has gone, the new is here" (2 Cor. 5:17 [NIV]).*

Surveyor 1 received and implemented the off-course instructions, and completed its intended journey to the great joy of the men and women who conceived the spacecraft, created and equipped it with all it needed, and guided the mission to its safe landing.

Sadly, Surveyor 2 failed to reach its destination due to a mid-course correction failure. The craft hurtled to the moon out of control because it failed to obey the command for midcourse correction. It crashed on the moon at high speed destroying itself . There was sorrow among the creators of Surveyor 2, but there was nothing that could be done after the spacecraft failed to carry out the mid-course correction command.

A MID-COURSE CORRECTION FOR A FRIEND

Gary was a colleague of mine, and a friend as well. It was a Sunday evening when his wife Ann called. "Dick, I'm worried about him. He got in his car and headed for town. I don't know what to do. He says you are his friend at work and I am worried." I told her I would try to locate him.

To find his vehicle at night was a challenge. But on a second trip to the general area where he might have gone, I spotted his car parked in front of a restaurant-bar. While parking my car I asked myself, "How should I approach him?" He wasn't waiting for, or expecting me. However, I did care about him. Beyond that, we were friends. I did not know what was going on inside him, but I was willing to push through the awkwardness of taking a seat across from him while he was eating.

Predictably, Gary looked up and said "What are you doing here?" I responded, "I'm here Gary, because I am your friend." He kept eating, not wanting to look my way. I said "Gary, Ann called me and said that you left the house under a lot of stress. I don't know anything more than that, but she is clearly worried about you." The silence was awkward but I had to give him the space he needed, hoping that somewhere along the line, he would let me help him shoulder whatever he was carrying. I asked him if he was going home that evening. He said no, that he had booked a room in a local motel so he could sort things out in his own mind. I suggested he finish his meal, and then we could go back to his room to talk. He agreed.

Conversation at the motel started slowly. Gary struggled, searching for words. Then looking at me, he got it out. "I'm troubled within, and I can't take it anymore." After some awkward and disconnected moments, it came out. It was hard for him but he was able to tell me that he had made a huge mistake in his life, and the secret he had buried had been eating at him ever since. I tried to read between the lines and then asked him if he had reached out to anyone for help. He admitted that he had been seeing a psychiatric counselor. After a long pause, I asked him if his counselor had been helpful. There was more silence. Then he said, "He told me that I should shove it under the rug, and get on with my life."

I wrote earlier in this memoir how my own secretive double life had caused great suffering in my mind, a suffering that almost killed me. I was feeling great compassion for my friend and told him the essence of my life story, one in which I tried to live a double life and the grief it caused me. I told him about the grace of God which had rescued me from a mental institution and changed my life in mid-course through a tangible encounter with Jesus Christ. Gary could not hold it in any longer. The emotions that had been bottled up and buried for so long were now out in the open. I sat in silence until the river had run its course.

Gary had been attending a local denominational church, so he was not unfamiliar with the Gospel found in Jesus' teachings. As I spoke, I felt the power of the Holy Spirit filling the room where we were talking. I assured him that Jesus was not condemning his failure, but offering him the only path to forgiveness, restoration and freedom. I suggested that Gary let Jesus have whatever was under the rug. I assured him that Jesus' death on the cross was for the purpose of taking upon Himself all our sin and double mindedness, even our broken vows. Jesus, the Son of God knew every failure in our lives, and it was for that reason that He came into our human experience to pay our debt of sin and set us on a new path of freedom.

Soon we knelt by his bed and Gary opened his heart completely to Jesus, confessed his sin, and received the freedom of a heart made clean and the salvation that was now his by faith. I assured Gary that God was preparing a way for him to share his burden with his wife and that God would be faithful to him and bring healing to his wife and eventually to his marriage. I promised Gary that I would pray daily for God to direct his steps. He trusted God with his relationship with Ann and confessed to her what had been under the rug, asking for her forgiveness. In due time, they both were attending a Bible study at their church. Gary had experienced a mid-course correction in his life, and the joy of moving forward to a new destination was as real as was the Surveyor Spacecraft which had gotten off-course but was redirected to bring it to its intended destination. Gary and I knew that language well, and the appropriateness of it was powerful since we shared in the success of the flight of Surveyor 1.

God is faithful! My commitment to follow Jesus Christ had led me to a world view and a life experience which was beyond expectation. I was walking in the way that He had shown me. My faith, however, was about to receive a personal test.

6

A TEST OF FAITH

I unexpectedly received a letter with an impressive looking return address from a hiring firm in Hollywood. "We have a client on the East Coast who is very interested in talking with you about an employment opportunity we believe you might want to consider." The letter did not disclose the name of the company, but it was clearly written to pique my curiosity and to increase the possibility of a response from me. Frankly I could not conceive of an opportunity more challenging than my current job and friends at JPL not to mention the perks of living in sunny Southern California! However, the inquiry did generate some questions in my mind. Out of sheer curiosity I succumbed and answered the letter. A week later I received an invitation from an East Coast aerospace company, AVCO Space Systems Division, to visit their facilities and consider employment opportunities they believed would challenge me. Out of curiosity, I accepted the invitation, fully realizing that I could also have a visit with my family living in the Boston area.

After visiting the company, meeting some of the people I might be working with, and learning of the aerospace programs they were working on, I returned to my desk at JPL somewhat depressed! My prayer now included a new phrase. "Lord, you're kidding right?"

The fact was, I was still enjoying my dream job at JPL. The mountains of California had become a great place for camping.

Lake Tahoe was a jewel. With the desert and trips to San Diego on the south and Santa Barbara on the north, who would want to move back to the cold North East? I was about to take a test for which I was not prepared. Could it be, that God who healed me, who had led me through my education and finally to JPL, was now leading me back to the Northeast? If so, was I willing to pick up and leave? Was I willing to put God's purposes ahead of mine? If I did leave JPL, it would be a true exercise in faith. No increase in salary or position could compete with the grace of the One who had brought me back from the shadow of death. I believed that the new life I had in Christ was not my own, but a life to be lived in obedience to Him who showed merciful love to me. That confession was about to be challenged. Beyond receiving the love of God was the call of obedience to follow Him as He led the way.

"Whoever serves me; must follow me and wherever I am my servant will be also. My Father will honor the one who serves me" (John 12:26).

I received a letter of invitation to join the Antenna Systems Department of AVCO systems division as a Research Engineer, which included an increase in salary and the opportunity to grow with the company. I was requested to give my answer in two weeks.

Kathy and I discussed the options and prayed for guidance. In decisions like this, she has been a sincere and loving support throughout the years. She has always expressed her concern that I do what I felt God was leading me to, and whatever that was, she was on board. In return, I felt that she needed to know my thoughts and that we would pray concerning these kinds of issues. She emulates to this day the spirit of Ruth in the Old Testament.

"But Ruth replied, 'Don't urge me to leave you or turn back from you. Where you go I will go, and where you stay I will stay. Your people will be my people and your God my God'" (Ruth 1:16).

The deadline for a decision was closing in on me, yet I could not seem to make that decision. I told one of my co-workers, a fellow believer, of the decision that I was faced with and asked for his prayers. On the morning of "decision day" I went to work and took a few minutes in the rest room to read some Scripture and pray. Still, I had no answer. I walked out of the rest room, still undecided, and made my way down the hall way. My friend who had been praying for me came out of his office as I was passing by and said, "Dick, have you made a decision yet?" I looked at him squarely and said "I am leaving. I've decided to accept AVCO's offer and move back to the East Coast."

My own ears could not believe what had just come out of my mouth, yet a tangible peace settled over me. I somehow knew that it was the right decision. I became willing to leave my "dream" job of a few years behind, in order to see what God's plan was for the next phase of my life and that of my wife and future family. A sense of inner peace has always been a sure sign of God's presence in following His plan in my life. I called Kathy and told her that I had decided to take AVCO's offer. As I expected, she affirmed me in my decision. We both received the hope of the Apostle Paul who said:

"May the God of hope fill you with all joy and peace as you trust in him, so that you may overflow with hope by power of the Holy Spirit" (Rom. 15:13).

I sent an acceptance letter to AVCO and scheduled a meeting with the Section Chief (who had welcomed me to JPL a few years back) to tell him that I had made a decision to take a position at a company back on the East Coast. He wished to know if there was anything he could do to persuade me to stay. I told him the basis of my decision, which was to follow God's leading in my life. I assured him that my time at JPL was extremely rewarding and thanked him for the opportunity to start my career working on the Surveyor flight to the moon. We agreed on a time table for my leaving and he wished me well.

Admittedly, there were a few of my colleagues that wondered if I had traded relocation to the Northeast in exchange for a big raise in salary. In fact, the cost of living in the new location neutralized the increase. God's purpose was displayed very early upon my arrival at the new company. I learned that along with working on interplanetary aerospace programs, I would also be working in an "Outpatient Clinic".

7
MINISTRY IN THE WORKPLACE

Returning to the Northeast was an exercise in faith. I was learning the implications of trusting in God for situations I had not known before. I had already been blessed beyond expectations when I was given the opportunity to participate in the flight of Surveyor 1, NASA's early exploration of the moon. Now, I was given the opportunity to expand that exploration to the planets Venus and Jupiter and work on other cutting-edge research projects.

While having lunch with a colleague one day, we were talking about the excitement of being at the forefront of space exploration in our work. At one point I said to my friend, "You know I would do all this work even if they didn't pay me!" We laughed in agreement. It was understood of course there were mortgage payments, grocery bills and other needs in our families so the weekly check was appreciated. But the sentiment was real. Honestly, coming to work early and leaving late was not a requirement, but a love for my work. However, a balance was necessary as I did have a family whose support and love was deeply appreciated and they still remain the most significant part of my life.

THE OUTPATIENT CLINIC

My work assignments at AVCO were challenging and creative. My colleagues and I were often involved in what we called "Phase

A" studies of spacecraft communications systems, specifically the design and development of advanced space craft antennas.

One day upon arriving at work, I was approaching the building when I looked up and "saw" a sign over the entrance doors that read "Outpatient Clinic." There was no physical sign over the door, but in my mind I did see it (in the Spirit, I assume). I asked the Lord, "What was that about?" as I made my way to my office. Then in my mind, I definitely heard words that I could not have made up. "My son, I have people who walk in and out of these buildings five days a week, working eight hours a day; people who are hurting, fearful, and worried about many things, and some of those families are falling apart. I want to heal them." I pondered this for the rest of that day. In my daily prayers which followed, I asked the Lord what He wanted me do concerning the "Outpatient Clinic." He led me to his Word, where I received this written answer:

> *"But in your hearts revere Christ as Lord. Always be prepared to give an answer to everyone who asks you to give the reason for the hope that you have. But do this with gentleness and respect" (1 Peter 3:15).*

Was it a coincidence that shortly after my inquiry concerning that sign over the door, I met a colleague from another department and discovered that we both had faith in Jesus Christ? We were like two boats in a large body of water that discovered we were rowing in the same direction!

My new friend Robert and I met for lunch several times and realized we shared something else in common; a desire to gather others of like faith for a weekly Bible study. The two of us met once a week during our forty-five minute lunch period. It felt however that we were holding a place for something undefined in the near future, something that would take time and prayer to develop. In the meantime, we kept meeting and my work assignments were becoming more and more demanding and challenging.

TESTS FOR WHAT WAS COMING

A research project allowed me to do some theoretical studies of advanced antenna systems for space applications. The work resulted in an opportunity to present the findings in a technical paper at a gathering of the Institute of Electrical Engineers (IEE) in London.

The meeting took place over a period of three days. Friday was a free day before boarding my return flight on Saturday morning. The free day offered an opportunity for some sightseeing. I walked around "London town" enjoying some of the traditional sights, like the changing of the guard at Buckingham Palace. Kathy reminds me that it must have been exciting since I took about twenty shots of the palace guards framed over the bald head of a man who was standing in front of me!

After enjoying an evening meal in a London restaurant, I decided to take a walk around town before checking out of my hotel for the return trip to the US. I soon found myself in a strange place; the "entertainment" sector of the city. Alone and tired after three days of meetings, and killing time, I was now facing "storefronts" with "messengers" outside trying to persuade me that I would like what I found inside their dimly lit business establishment, and that I should come in and check things out. My pace quickened as I passed more of these shops offering discount prices and other benefits to come into their premises. Clearly I had walked right into the sex-entertainment district of London.

I crossed over to the other side of the street to make my way back to the main street where my hotel was located. While walking back, there were several theaters blatantly advertising the pornographic nature of the films being shown. Although there were no sidewalk peddlers for these theaters, the marquees and billboards took their place and offered very strong pitches concerning what was going on inside. At one of these theaters I stopped and looked at the advertising. While looking on, I heard a voice speak to me in persuasive terms. The voice sounded foreign. "You know there will be people with whom you will want to share your faith but you won't be able to relate to them because you don't have much in common with them. Why not take this opportunity to see what they see so that you can relate to them when you share your Christ with them. Go ahead; one time is not going to hurt." Then, as if a counter reminder, I recalled a few verses of a hymn which I had learned as a child in the church in which I was raised:

> *I would be true for there are those who trust me;*
> *I would be pure, for there are those who care;*
> *I would be strong, for there is much to suffer;*
> *I would be brave, for there is much to dare.*

> *I would be faithful through each passing moment;*
> *I would be constantly in touch with God;*
> *I would be strong to follow where He leads me;*
> *I would have faith to keep the path Christ trod.*

My family flashed through my mind. How could I do such a thing? I had two boys whose Dad had led them to Jesus and a dear wife who had stood by me in every decision we made, and who believed me when I pledged those vows of love and faithfulness "until death we do part". How could I even think of betraying them?

I pulled myself away from the front of that theater and began to walk even more quickly, not slowing down until I had found my way back to my hotel. I realized I had just escaped a direct assault of the enemy. I had escaped a trap cleverly set in an atmosphere remote from home. I would discern much later that Satan knew what was ahead of me as I sought to represent Jesus in the workplace. He had planned this assault while I was thousands of miles from home, to isolate me and thwart the plans that God had in mind for my life.

On a subsequent occasion, I was scheduled to attend a conference at a southwestern university to familiarize myself with work being done in my area of spacecraft antenna system design. Except for accommodations, I was on my own for flight plans and meals. I was also instructed to contact the office organizing the event for any other information needed.

I had some questions, so I called the number provided. After my questions, I was quite surprised to learn that since the conference went over the weekend my contact offered to make some "connections" for me. Being a university town, there were non-advertised opportunities which he was willing to set up, and it would not cost me anything. Ah, but it could cost me everything! I didn't want to believe the kind of entertainment he was offering me but after more conversation, it became clear. He was willing to set me up with those willing to "service" guests at the conference.

To make sure I understood him, I asked more questions. I then told him that I was flatly not interested, that I was happily married, had two small sons, and my commitment to them and Jesus Christ, whom I serve, was lifelong. There was silence on the other end of the phone. He wished me well at the conference. That evening after dinner, I told Kathy about the phone call I had in connection with my planned trip west. I wanted her to know that she was the one to whom I had pledged my love until death we do part.

I learned that to be a servant of God in the workplace, we must be constantly on our guard and avoid compromise with the enemy who wants to divide our minds and hearts. Satan is clever and will weaken our resolve to follow Jesus so as to render us powerless in representing Him in the workplace. With subtle temptations he purposes to diminish the authenticity of our walk with Jesus, weaken the power of the Holy Spirit within, and thwart our effectiveness in representing Him to others.

AN INCREASE IN RESPONSIBILITY

A time came when the growth of our antenna research section contributed to the expansion of our organization. My immediate supervisor John, who had responsibility for leading a group of some fifty engineers and technicians, was promoted up to department manager. Shortly thereafter he called me into his office asking me if I would be interested in taking his former position as Section Chief. It meant that I would oversee the work of the engineers in the section while continuing to have projects of my own. I was honored that he would ask me and after prayerful consideration, I agreed and became Chief Engineer.

Several months later, John had to take time off due to sickness in his family. I learned from his secretary that John's wife had been hospitalized. Not knowing much more, I was genuinely concerned. I felt I could identify with his concerns for his wife due to my own struggle that led me to a new life. John returned to work after a few days and asked me into his office to give a report on the status of projects while he was away. After giving my report, I expressed my concern for his wife as well as hope that she would be well soon. He felt confident.

Our conversation deepened as I candidly conveyed my own struggle with hospitalization years earlier. In the privacy of his office, I told him of the darkness which I endured, including months of despair which ultimately became a turning point in my life. I spoke of the healing miracle that took place when Jesus Christ found me walking aimlessly in a field, in extreme loneliness and loss of hope. Not wanting to take the time at the office to tell him the full story, I brought the conversation to a close with an invitation to my home for dinner. He thanked me and indicated that he would come. We set a time for several days later. I stood to leave his office, encouraging him to read the Gospels, and at the door I said, "John, I don't want to simplify anything, but Jesus brought me real life. When I received Him into my life during those dark days, He set me free!" I left his office looking forward to a meeting at my home when we could talk some more.

In the meantime, I spent much time in prayer asking God to lead John and me in our upcoming conversation. I prepared myself by making a list of scriptures that spoke about the personal encounter we can have with God through Jesus. The day of our meeting, John called to tell me that he could not make it for dinner, but that he would still come albeit a bit later. Thirty minutes before his arrival I made my appeal to God asking him to give me clarity and the leading of His Spirit as I talked with my friend and supervisor. It seemed to me that the main purpose of our meeting was that John would find peace and hope through Jesus, who desired a personal relationship with him.

The door bell rang. I welcomed John in and after some small talk, asked him how his wife was doing. He did not answer me at first. He seemed happy to see me but anxious to tell me about something else. Instead he said, "Dick, do you remember what you said to me when you left my office last week?" I said, "Refresh my memory."

"You said, concerning Jesus, that when you received him into your life, he set you free, remember?"

I responded, "Yes, I remember."

John said, "Well, I went home and started reading the Gospels as you suggested. Then, in John 3:16 I read, 'God so loved the world, that He gave His only son, that whoever believes in Him, should not perish but have eternal life.' I put the Bible down, prayed and asked God to forgive me of my sin and be my Savior. Then I sensed that all my sins had been forgiven as I received Jesus into my life. Dick, he has set *me* free as well!"

I was at a loss for words—to say the least!

Wow! I was ready to take him through the Gospel for that very purpose, but God Himself accompanied John's reading and the Holy Spirit opened his eyes without any further help from me. I've learned that God is often just ahead of me. In the days following, it was apparent that his faith had taken root in his life. Although we related at the office in an organizational chart, we had a relationship with Christ that made us brothers.

I learned that in the workplace, a believer represents the love and compassion of Jesus to those who find themselves without answers for the issues of life. Indeed, the "sign over the door" of which I spoke earlier had revealed that there are people coming in and out of the building day after day, five days a week, and eight hours per day whose lives are hurting, and God does want to draw alongside them to heal them. It is through the Gospel and believers who sincerely follow Jesus that His grace and mercy find their way into the workplace.

A SPACE SHUTTLE RE-ENTRY CHALLENGE

Most of our business as an aerospace communications contractor was from the government, NASA, or from government subcontracts with private industry. Rockwell International was the contractor for the Space Shuttle Orbiter. A Request for Proposal (RFP) was sent out to industrial contractors including AVCO to solve a potential problem associated with the re-entry portion of the flight. During re-entry, the heat generated on the nose cone of the Orbiter might cause a condition preventing the radar landing system from functioning properly.

The proposal came at a time when our business load was slow. In fact, during the six months previous, my section experienced one of the most painful declines in business resulting in the need to cut back the work force to accommodate the realities.

When I took leadership over the Antenna Section, there were about thirty-five technical people including support staff. That number grew to about fifty-five. However, the time came when the government could no longer support the research and development activity and layoffs became numerous. When the bottom was reached, I had approximately twenty technical people left in place.

It was painful calling some very good engineers into my office only to tell them that our work load could no longer support the size of our staff. I witnessed grown men, accomplished in their technical expertise well up with tears in their eyes, when I informed them of their release. I had no reluctance to pray with some of them who had become friends as they sought employment elsewhere. I offered a letter of recommendation to several as they sought other employment.

The arrival of the Space Shuttle Request for Proposal (RFP) required that I assume responsibilities that I had not exercised before. I was designated as the prime contact with the engineers at Rockwell. It was my responsibility to acquaint Rockwell with AVCO's technical design and test capabilities, and involve myself with contract issues of cost and schedule details. In the end, with support from our remaining engineers and other technical support people, we generated a proposal which would address Rockwell's technical concerns and provide a cost proposal and schedule to accomplish the task.

Assigned the responsibility of Project Engineer, I felt I was in over my head, but had no choice. We were in desperate times. It was, however, an opportunity to trust God that His purpose would be represented in all I was being asked to do, and that He would be as faithful as He had been in the past.

I recall my feelings while walking alone into an introductory meeting at Rockwell in California. As I went around the table and exchanged greetings with their team, I greeted them in my heart in the name of Jesus, to remind myself inwardly to be open and available to God. It may be that somewhere along the way there might be someone who needed to hear about the One who could bring healing to their lives and families. The technical aspects of my visit were presented to give them the confidence that AVCO had the expertise and facilities to help them solve the Orbiter re-entry problem. I was soon on my way home via a flight from Los Angeles.

NO SLEEP ON A FLIGHT EAST

I was exhausted on my return trip to Boston. The pressure of doing something which I had no prior experience with was finally released. Just getting on the plane and adjusting a pillow seemed good to me. I recall taking my aisle seat and immediately plugging my headphones into the system for some music. The plane was quite full and the seat next to me was still empty. I was hoping it would stay that way, so I could stretch out and enjoy a cross country nap.

At the very last minute and with a full plane, except for the seat next to me, a woman of middle age was obviously stressed not being able to find her seat. I am thinking to myself, "No it cannot be this seat beside me!" But standing over me and checking her boarding pass, she declared the inevitable, "Oh yes, here is my seat!" I pulled off my headphones, rose up and let her take her seat, then quickly regained my relaxed position with the headphones back in place. After a few moments she leaned over and said "I need a drink! I am so nervous! I don't like to fly." I told her they wouldn't serve drinks until we were in the air. She said she was not only nervous, but upset. I sensed there was a rationale for her need for a drink. I asked her why she was upset, had she not flown before? She said, "I am upset about my daughter. I think she has joined a cult in Colorado." It appeared that my opportunity for a transcontinental nap was slowly evaporating.

Then God began to speak to me. "I know you're tired, but could you spend these last few hours talking with this person whose seat I have saved that she might sit next to you? Listen to her. Perhaps you could take a few more hours and engage with this woman whose heart is fearful."

As our plane lifted off, we were still talking about her daughter when I asked her what "cult" her daughter had joined. She responded, "I think they're called The Navigators." I then told her, much to her surprise, that I knew the organization she was concerned about. I assured her that she need not fear, because I believed that her daughter was in good hands. I told her that the Navigators ministry helps young people become leaders in representing Jesus to the world in which they live.

I asked her "May I tell you a personal story?" She nodded. I told her that when I was perhaps her daughter's age, I went through a crisis in my life. For the next twenty minutes or so, I told her of how Jesus revealed His love for me, and how He moved me to give my shattered life to Him for healing. As we talked she seemed to become introspective, curious and longing. I told her the story of Jesus ministering to the woman at the well in John's gospel. I had a New Testament with me and read the story to her. Jesus had asked the woman for a drink, but she felt she could not offer Him water, because Jesus was a Jew and she a Samaritan and culturally they did not socialize with each other. In her mind, He was asking her for something impossible. Jesus then said to her that if she really knew who she was talking to, she would ask Him for a drink, for those who drink the water He offers will never thirst again (John 4:13-14).

I suggested to her that her daughter had taken a drink from the well Jesus was offering, which was a well of spiritual water, designed to meet the needs of her daughters' thirsty heart. I explained that Jesus was speaking in that passage about the Holy Spirit who quenches spiritual thirst. I explained that millions of people down through the centuries have taken a drink from Jesus' well, and received peace, joy, and a new life. I knew this to be true because I had personally received the living water from the well of which Jesus spoke.

No longer concerned for her daughter, she started asking questions out of the pain in her own heart. I took her through several scriptures to ultimately show her that on the cross Jesus gave Himself so that through His resurrection, she could share in a new life with Him. Somewhere, high over the Midwest, she opened her heart to Jesus and, through prayer, received Him as her Savior. Now she would have much to share with her daughter, and I assured her that her daughter would be happy to hear that mom had received Jesus on a flight to Boston.

We enjoyed a Bible study together as we continued our flight. Then, as we were descending over the Boston area, she looked at me and said, "Oh my, I haven't had my drink!" I told her, "But you did have a drink; the one that Jesus offered you, remember? If you choose, you'll never have to depend on that other kind of drink again. The water that Jesus gives you is for eternal life." As we taxied to the gate, she gave me her contact information. I kept my promise to send her some material the very next day that would help her grow in her newly found faith in Jesus.

A YELLOW CAB FROM THE AIRPORT

Facing a 45 minute drive from Logan Airport to my home in Burlington, I thought this time I might finally take the nap I was longing to have. I retrieved my luggage and went to the curb for a yellow cab. Most of the cabs had customers already. Finally, I approached a driver who rolled down his window while moving a big black cigar from side to side in his mouth. I asked what the fare to Burlington would be. We agreed on a price and as he was loading my luggage, I began to wonder if I should be taking this cab. This cabbie made me nervous; he looked intimidating, and in my mind could have passed as a Boston gangster, or perhaps a member of the Mafia! As we drove out of the taxi lane into main traffic, I kept wondering about him. I rationalized everything by telling myself that he must be reliable. After all, he was driving a Yellow Cab! I tried to relax.

I had driven the route from Logan airport to Burlington myself, but I had never gone the way this driver was taking me. We were hitting parts of Boston I had never seen and I had lived near Boston most of my life. It was late in the evening and one-way back alley streets, some not well lit, did nothing to decrease my uneasiness.

The driver opened the window separating the customer from the driver and said. "So, you are on your way home this evening?" I said "Yes, and it has been a long day." Then he said, "You know, I am amazed at how many people I pick up who are fearful." I asked myself what that statement had to do with driving me home. Looking at him it was easy to imagine anyone in this cab feeling some fear. Why did he just speak about fear? The darkened back streets of Boston were not allowing me to relax. Then the driver decided to tell me a story. "Recently, I picked up a woman, who refused to get out of my cab for fear of going up to her apartment alone. I had to convince her by telling her I would not move my cab until she was safe inside her front door." Really, I thought? He is telling me that a woman passenger wants to stay in his cab for fear of going up to her darkened apartment? I guess it was all relative for her. But his story caused me to loosen up a little and listen to my own thoughts.

There was silence for several minutes. Then I recognized that we were about to turn onto Route 93 North which led to my home in Burlington. I started to relax, realizing we had taken a short cut through Boston. I wish it had been during the daylight hours, I may have recognized some of the streets, but I doubt it. Finally I said, "You know, when you were telling me about that woman who was fearful of getting out of your cab, I was reminded of a time when I was stricken with fear." I then shared my story of how I almost threw my life away, ending up in a psychiatric hospital with fear a constant companion. I told him that God intervened, healed me, and gave me a new reason for living.

He was listening, intently turning his head toward the open window between front and back seat so he could hear above the noise of traffic. I finished my story just as we were pulling up in front of my house. I then asked the driver, "Do you have a few more minutes? Perhaps you would like to know that you can be assured of God's love for you." He said "Sure, come on up to the front seat so I can hear." I joined him in the front seat, and began to share with him the message of the Gospel by way of a tract that was popular at the time. As I was explaining the death of Jesus on the cross and its meaning, I looked over at him and noticed tears streaming down his hardened face. It was totally unexpected. His cigar had gone out, and it just seemed to be hanging there as the tears flowed past. The evidence that his heart was being touched by the Holy Spirit working salvation in him was clear.

With his permission I prayed with him and led him in a prayer of repentance and faith. He looked stunned and became a man of few words. The tears continued to flow. I encouraged him to start a daily relationship with God, by reading the Bible and talking with Him in prayer. I gave him a booklet to help him and suggested that while he waited for customers at Logan International, he might use that time to talk with God. I promised I would be praying for him in the days to come. As he left the curb he turned around at the intersection just up the street and came back past the house, waving the booklet, and yelling out the window "Thank you, thank you!" It was an affirmation that God had indeed touched his heart. I went into the house to my waiting wife and told her to sit down; that God had just performed a miracle in a taxi cab!

As God was teaching my new friend in the cab, so He was ministering to me as well. As I reflected later on the whole event, I sensed in my Spirit that I was being taught never to judge anyone from external appearances. I went on to read from 1 Samuel:

"But the Lord said to Samuel, 'Do not consider his appearance or his height, for I have rejected him. The Lord does not look at the things people look at. People look at the outward appearance, but the Lord looks at the heart'" (1 Sam. 16:7).

The heart of this taxi driver was empty and longing. I would have never guessed it. I almost let outward circumstances block me from sharing what he needed to hear. As I look back on that experience, I confess that for the first fifteen minutes of our ride through Boston, I felt the need to be quiet and just take the ride home. If he hadn't started the conversation, I might have remained silent. I learned that night that in the workplace such as in a taxi cab, I had to resist giving into a spirit of intimidation and not be the judge of anyone based on outward appearances.

"For God has not given us a spirit of fear, but of power and of love and of a sound mind" (2 Tim. 1:7).

Fear disables the gifts within us, causes us to back off and wait for another day. For some there might not be another day. However, for this taxi driver who was looking for life with an empty heart, it was his day!

ON THE JOB TRAINING IN THE WORKPLACE

Back in the office following the trip to California, I outlined the tasks necessary to generate the technical, cost and schedule proposal to be submitted to Rockwell. After that trip, I was about to watch events unfold that I could not have imagined.

Plasma physicist, Dr. Bob Jantrea became the principle investigator for a solution to the Orbiter re-entry problem. It was his work that gave some direction as to what the design of the radar antennas on the nose of the orbiter might look like. Models were configured and tested in our antenna test facilities. During this preliminary design effort Bill, one of our draftsmen, was assigned the responsibility for generating drawings describing potential physical designs which I was to take to Rockwell for review.

On the Friday before I was to leave for Rockwell, Dr. Bob and I went to view the progress of the drawings as they were being finished and discovered that a serious error had rendered the drawings unacceptable. Corrections had to be made. I informed Bill that he would have to come in on Saturday, his day off, to make the necessary corrections. I also told him I would come in as well. The corrections were made, and the drawings accompanied me to Rockwell as planned.

Upon my return, Dr. Bob came into my office quite perturbed concerning what had happened with the draftsman before I left for Rockwell the previous Friday. "Herskind", he said, "what makes you tick?" He continued. "The issue with Bill last Friday … if I were you I would have fired the guy! He would have been out of here. But you stayed calm, told him he had to work on his day off, and that you would forfeit your day off as well. Again, I don't understand; what makes you tick?" Sensing that the Holy

Spirit was in the middle of his outburst, I answered, "Bob, do you really want to know?" I had been praying for some time that God would give me favor with Dr. Bob. He had a brilliant mind and was a likable guy. It occurred to me that the opportunity was presenting itself in Bob's question.

I invited him back to my office and shuffled through some papers in my desk drawer looking for a letter written in response to the question: Can God be known personally, and if so how? The letter was written by a business man who had been asked by a colleague how one can find peace with God. I found a copy and suggested that Dr. Bob might be interested in reading it. If so, we could have lunch to discuss it further. Dr. Bob took the letter and went back to his office.

The following week he came to me and placed the letter on my desk with the comment: "That was very interesting." I asked him what he had found interesting. "Well at the end of the letter, the writer talked about how one could have a relationship with God through Jesus Christ. In the letter was a prayer which, one could pray if there was a sincere desire to receive Jesus Christ by way of the Holy Spirit." Then Dr. Bob looked at me and said, "Well, I prayed that prayer, and I believe something has been happening within me."

I was surprised by his comment. Here was a man who spent most of his life looking at complex mathematical equations with an equal sign in the middle, telling me that he needed no further proof; that what the letter conveyed was true. I told Dr. Bob that I was happy for his discovery, and then asked him how he knew that something was happening in his heart. He showed me his thumb which recently had met the force of a hammer. He explained that he had been working on his house with some of his friends when he struck his thumb. He then volunteered the following: "Dick, I know that something has happened to me through that prayer because if I had hit my thumb before this change in my heart, the whole neighborhood would have known it through my usual colorful language. I simply yelled a high volume ouch." He said that was a miracle.

We agreed to continue with our desire to talk over lunch. We enjoyed a time of sharing the mystery of walking with Jesus in a real relationship. At one point I said, "So Bob, do you still want to know what makes me tick?" He countered with a smile "No, I have finally figured you out."

In the days which followed, it became obvious that Dr. Bob's life was changed. I offered him a study in discipleship that would be very helpful to him and volunteered to meet with him to help him grow in his new relationship with God. He expressed interest but wanted to do it himself, which he did. He said he would come to see me if he had any questions. Indeed, his heart had been changed.

THE PROPOSAL OPENS A DOOR

Our work on the proposal for Rockwell International continued. Dr. Bob's theoretical work on the physics of the interaction of microwave signals through plasma attracted the interest of others and created an opportunity for Bob to explain his work at a technical meeting at AVCO.

On the day of Dr. Bob's presentation, we sat together in the front row of the meeting room. Some NASA and government officials were making comments prior to the presentation. My attention was centered on Dr. Bob, and I offered a silent prayer that God would give him clarity of thinking and a skillful presentation on the findings of his theoretical analysis. While I was praying in my heart, Dr. Bob grabbed my arm, leaned over to me and whispered "Hey, you know what I read this morning in the Bible? I read that God knows the numbers of hairs on our heads, and God knows when a sparrow falls to the ground. That is so cool!" (*ref.* Matt. 10:29-30). So, while I was praying, he was excited over what he had read in the Bible about hairs on his head and birds that fall from the sky! God was present and Dr. Bob's presentation was excellent, as usual.

I was discovering that God was more than faithful to His call to serve Him in the workplace. If I would be diligent in using whatever gifts He had given me for the work I was doing and the people I was working with, He would work through my weaknesses and bring glory to Himself.

ROCKWELL VISITS AVCO

Our preparation and response to the Request For Proposal started several months of technical analysis, cost proposal, and program schedule considerations. A draft was submitted and generated a desire at Rockwell to visit our facilities and evaluate our capacity to solve the Orbiter re-entry problem.

I had not generated a full technical cost proposal, ever. But the time had come to reveal to Rockwell our cost analysis. We gathered in a conference room, with three engineering and two finance personnel from Rockwell and a similar number of representatives from AVCO. I was presenting an overview of our cost proposal when the lead financial officer of the group asked me from across the table what the symbol on my tie-tack represented. Then, as it was an interruption, I looked down to recall what I had worn that day. It was the ICKTHUS, the fish symbol that early Christians used to identify themselves to one another. Holding my tie up for a moment I responded by saying, "You mean this? This is a symbol of the faith of the early Christian community and represents my faith in Jesus Christ as well." I suggested that at our scheduled dinner at a Boston restaurant that evening we could talk some more about it, if he so wished. I then refocused on the task at hand.

Pier Four, a favorite Boston restaurant, was the location of our dinner with the Rockwell folks. While waiting for our food, we talked about the Red Sox, the historical monuments which told the story of the Revolutionary war, and many other topics of interest. Tom, the leader of the Rockwell team then said, "Well about your tie tack. So you are a Christian?" I said yes and gave a very brief testimony of how I came to follow Jesus. The Bible then took center stage as some of the men questioned its reliability and whether it was relevant to our time in history. The inquiry was honest, and I did make some comments. I have learned, however, that it's more fruitful to talk about the person of Jesus since the Bible is all about Him anyway.

The discussion lasted a good hour and we could have continued longer. One of the men said, "This has been a great conversation. I have attended Bible studies back in California, but my experience is that Christians don't have answers to my questions. I believe I could become a Christian if I had a study to go to like we have had tonight." I assured him that God is not limited in space and time, and He is able to meet us anywhere and answer any questions through His Spirit leading our thoughts. We did have a full day ahead of us in the morning, so they retired to their hotel and I drove home. It wasn't long after Rockwell's visit to AVCO that we formally submitted our proposal.

About four weeks later, I received a call from Rockwell's contract office with the words: "Congratulations, you have won the contract!" I rocked back in my office chair and wanted to say "Really?" but I checked myself and said, "Well that is good news!"

The caller went on to say that he and one of their finance people would like to take me out to breakfast before meeting with our contracts department so we set the date. During our breakfast, the finance representative asked me if I knew why Rockwell had picked AVCO as contractor to support the Orbiter landing radar antenna study. I said "Well, I hope that means you believe we can do the job." He continued, "Well that was a given, but there were other factors." He then spoke of the openness and honesty with which we conducted the cost proposal.

"We were impressed with how open you were in sharing with us how you arrived at the expected costs," he said. "We usually have to dig for the information; you just put it out there. Furthermore," he went on, "our team felt there was something genuine about you, that you were open and honest. Your personal approach to our team was well received." I don't know what stimulated that last sentence. Did the guys from dinner that night tell them about our Bible study? I'll never know. Yet I did take a personal interest in their team, because I believed that God had an interest in them as well. Jesus did much of His ministry in the workplace; the outpatient clinic of his day.

ANATOMY OF A WIN

At AVCO all contract proposals, whether won or lost, were debriefed for the marketing department. These meetings sought to gain understanding of the strengths and weaknesses of our RFP submissions. This again was a new thing for me. Having won the job, however, made it easier since I could be the bearer of good news. The meeting was mandatory for all marketing personnel, so the room was filled. I started by telling them that this was a new experience for me, but that I welcomed it as an opportunity to learn and to serve the people that were looking to us for expertise in solving a particular problem.

The first part of my presentation was to outline what the customer was looking to have us do for them. I shared our understanding of a solution to the problem and how we created a technical analysis, and a cost basis and time schedule for accomplishing the task. Each of these topics became the major input to the debriefing. Time was allowed for question and answers, and my supporting team was present to help when their technical expertise was needed.

For me, the most challenging part of the review, was describing how I approached the men and women from Rockwell with our proposal. I said that people share much in common in life. We all have our work to do, our families to feed, and our lives outside the workplace. Often however, our work is affected by what is going on in our private lives. Our tendency is to present the best side of who we are, while struggling inwardly with many personal issues. I told our marketing department that I wanted to leave the Rockwell team with the sense that we were there to support their project with a strong commitment.

I shared a short testimony of how faith in Jesus Christ had given me a whole new direction in life and a love for people in general. I wanted that love to be sensed by the customer, not overtly but in the way that I presented our desire to add our expertise to solve their problem.

By this time the fifty or so people at the meeting were exhibiting body language that ranged from "I can't believe what I am hearing", to "I thought this was a marketing meeting", while others were sitting forward on their seats wanting to hear more.

I also told them of the spontaneous Bible study I had with six of them at the Pier Four restaurant in Boston and how that came about. I told them how my "tie-tack story" had started it all when we were in conference concerning the cost proposal. That led their team leader at supper to ask again about my tie-tack, which allowed me to share perspectives on faith. At the end of an hour, I shared how one of their engineers said that he had attended Bible studies in California, but people couldn't answer his questions. He said "I think with another study like this, I could become a Christian." Finally, I told the marketing group what had been conveyed to me at breakfast by a Rockwell contract representative. While they affirmed that our technical approach was solid and we had the facilities, they also said that a trust factor was generated among them. I was told that was huge for them. They not only trusted our technical work, but the transparency with which we conducted our cost proposal convinced them that they could trust AVCO with all aspects of the contract. The marketing meeting ended with a sigh of relief from some, but generated conversation from others.

Echoes of that marketing meeting were heard a few months later at the company Christmas party sponsored by the marketing department. Kathy and I went early so we could have some conversations with people before their alcoholic "medications" set in. At one point, a gentleman approached me, and with slurred speech and a glass in his hand, said: "Herskind that was the best marketing report I ever heard." With the help of what he was drinking, I took his comments as an honest personal opinion.

A BIBLE STUDY IN THE WORKPLACE?

My department manager John and I were having a conversation over lunch one day, when I asked him what he thought about starting a Bible study during the lunch hour once a week. The study with Robert, which I mentioned earlier, did not continue. It just wasn't God's timing. But John and I recognized that there were photography clubs, clubs that tracked the stock market, and clubs with other varying interests, so why not a Bible Study Club? Recognizing that such a group might be looked on with favor by the Human Resources department, we made an appointment with them to explore the idea and to reserve a conference room weekly for a "brown bag" lunch and Bible study. Only one question was asked of us. "Are you representing a cult in this request?" We responded emphatically with a "no" and explained that the group would be inter-denominational, making it available to anyone who wanted to participate, and that John and I represented the Protestant and Catholic traditions. With that, permission was granted and a conference room assigned.

In a short period of time, there were people coming with their lunches to engage in a study of the life and teachings of Jesus as proclaimed in the Gospels. At one point the group numbered between fifteen and twenty weekly.

FOR SOME, THE TIME IS NOW!

Charlie, a middle aged man, became a regular attendee at the study. He was very quiet, and chose to sit against the wall where a few others also sat. The rest sat around the conference table. No one really knew very much about him.

After one study, Charlie followed me back to my office, and asked if we could talk. He said he had been listening for several weeks about Jesus and wanted to know more. I was running late in preparations for a technical meeting which I was to lead and had about twenty minutes to finish my preparations, eat my lunch and listen to Charlie. He seemed nervous and led me to believe that I needed to talk with him now and not later. As we talked, I sensed that Charlie wanted a personal relationship with

Jesus. I explained Jesus' work on the cross and how His death and resurrection opened the way for us to know him personally. Charlie appeared very receptive and anxious to receive God's love for him. At my invitation he prayed, opening his heart to Jesus. He asked for forgiveness of his sin and invited God to take up residence in his life. He appeared to be relieved as he looked up at me with a sense of wonder in what he had just discovered.

I suggested to Charlie that we get together in the next week or so to help him establish a personal discipline of seeking a deep relationship with Jesus through personal Bible study and prayer. He agreed, left my office, and I ran off to my meeting five minutes late. Despite my concern about my tardiness, I was the first one to arrive! However, I never saw Charlie again. I learned a few days after he had left my office that he had suffered a massive heart attack and died. I was shocked. I realized how close I had come to denying Charlie the hunger in his heart, when he had only a few days to live. God always finds a way to heal an aching soul searching for life. The question for me has become: whose schedule is the operating one—mine or God's?

SERMONS FROM SCIENCE

Our Bible study group became acquainted with a series of films produced by the Moody Bible Science Institute in Chicago, Illinois. The film series was shown at the World's fair in New York in 1964-5, and later in Montreal's Expo '67 and the 1974 Spokane World's Fair. Sermons from Science are a series of 30 minute films which demonstrate fascinating truths about the natural world and conclude with assertions of a supernatural creation. At the end of each movie, a five minute summary points to God as the creator and His self-revelation in Jesus Christ. Over the duration of the fair, this series had an attendance of one million visitors at a pavilion created for the showing of these films.

I knew of these films. John and I thought that the Bible study group might be interested in seeing a few of them, with the idea of sponsoring them at a larger showing in the company auditorium with approval from Human Resources. After viewing them at the Bible study group, the group embraced the idea of sponsoring a series of six of these films to be shown as proposed. The purpose was to provide a spiritual connection to the science and engineering that we as employees were doing every day. Our purpose was not to recruit for our weekly study but to plant seeds of faith in those who were wrestling with the unspoken questions of life. Perhaps some would be represented in the Outpatient Clinic.

Did sponsoring this series make any difference? Only God knows. Did our Bible study grow in attendance? There were a few who joined us in our weekly study. However, there was one upper management person who was seen sitting in the back of the auditorium each week. Subsequently, about a year later, I would come by his office for an unrelated purpose. A seed, which had been incubating for a while, burst forth in an incredible "chance" encounter in his office, but more on that later.

NOT EVERYONE WILL FOLLOW

Jesus' ministry in the workplace did not result in success with everyone following Him. For example Judas, the most notorious one, claimed to be a follower but later turned on Jesus and betrayed Him. Consequently, filled with agony, he committed suicide. Others, like the rich young ruler, found that selling all he had to follow Jesus was too costly. But to others, like the sick and lonely, and business people like Matthew the tax collector and John the fisherman, as well as many common folk of the day, following Jesus led to eternal life believing that He was the promised Messiah.

Jose was a good engineer. He worked in my engineering section, and was not a person of faith, nor did he have any interest in spiritual things. Knowing that spiritual things were important to me, he was secure enough in his own atheistic thoughts to poke at me now and then, pointing out to me "fallacies of faith" and the questionable reliability of such an ancient book as the Bible. I liked Jose. It was evident however, that Jose could not believe since the Bible to him was an ancient philosophical book like many others.

It happened that Jose got very sick and was out of the office for several days. I learned through others that he was in the hospital with a condition which was unidentified to us. I decided to take a lunch hour to visit him.

The expression on his face as I walked into his hospital room indicated that he was confused as to why I, his supervisor, would be at all interested in him outside of the office. "What are you doing here?" he asked. I told him that I had heard he was sick and just wanted to let him know that the guys and gals at the office wished him a quick recovery. I told him I had been praying that he would recover fully, and quickly rejoin his family at home and his colleagues back at the office. My time with him was only fifteen minutes or so, as I thought I should give him time to rest. As I was leaving, I sensed he did not know whether to thank me or have a discussion of the questionable value of the prayers I had offered on his behalf. Jose eventually returned to work and things returned to normal, until several months later.

One afternoon shortly before the end of the work day, Jose handed me his resignation. He explained that he had accepted a position in another company. He was a good engineer and had contributed much to our research projects. Although disappointed that he was leaving us, we had a going-away party for him at a local restaurant. That evening, he came to me privately and said "Dick, I understand now what you are about. Your visit to the hospital when I was sick caused me to believe that for you, faith is a living reality, and I do appreciate your caring for me. I, however, cannot believe." That evening was the last I saw of Jose.

> *"For God so loved the world that he gave his one and only Son, that whoever believes in him shall not perish but have eternal life" (John 3:16).*

I am persuaded that most people in their hearts wish they could believe. However their defenses against faith have to do with investments they have made in the pursuit of the material world and the inability to let go of themselves as the final authority for living life. Deep down they want to believe, because it is part of their spiritual DNA. But for them it appears costly, which it is. Jesus did say that those who were to follow Him, should pick up their cross and follow Him. The cross was a vivid symbol of death in Jesus' day. His invitation today is to live a new, empowered life in Him. This is a step too big for many. How grateful I am that God found me in an empty field crying out for His mercy and love.

THE VENUS CONNECTION

Jerry was an antenna systems technician. I assigned him to work with me on a study project concerning a possible spacecraft journey to the surface of the planet Venus. The challenge was to design an antenna which would allow communications through a very hostile Venusian atmosphere to the surface where the temperature is 900 degrees Fahrenheit. On its descent the antenna had to communicate with the mother ship in orbit around Venus. The antenna could not take up much space; it had to be of minimum weight and survive the intense heat. Those design specifications brought Jerry and I together on a feasibility study that would provide some answers.

As I walked to the antenna test facility, I thought of the many past conversations with Jerry; conversations about Jesus and God's plan of salvation. We were always respectful of each other. Inevitably however, Jerry always found a way to take my words and define them in naturalistic terms. If we were talking about love, he would speak of love in terms of activity in the brain. Love for Jerry was nothing more than a combination of neurons flashing in our brains in response to some external stimulus of mind and body resulting in a feeling of love. Jerry always had an answer based on his understanding of interactions in the natural world.

After a few weeks of conceiving design options, I had Jerry oversee the fabrication of a test model and run some "first look" measurements to see what possibilities existed. Jerry completed a set of tests and summoned me to the lab to take a look at some interesting preliminary results.

The measurements looked promising. I glanced at Jerry and the antenna model, and the thought came to me that the antenna we were seeking might in fact be designed, land on Venus, function for a brief time, and go silent forever. I considered my colleague and friend and in my mind acknowledged that he was wonderfully designed and was created to live forever in God's presence. But would his natural mind take him there? Where would he be at the end of his flight through life?

I don't know to this day, whether Jerry was able to overcome his naturalistic understanding of things and enter into the real world of faith. Nevertheless, I felt my role in Jerry's life was to respect him, care about him and pray for him rather than win a logical discussion. For me I leaned on the Scripture with the hope that sooner or later Jerry would understand. Did Jerry find his way to Jesus? I don't know. However, he had heard of the way to Jesus through conversations we had in the workplace.

"There is a way that appears to be right, but in the end it leads to death" (Prov. 16:25).

"Very truly I tell you, the one who believes has eternal life" (John 6:47).

While these experiences and many others were gifts of God to my life, there was another turn on the road ahead, and this was to be the sharpest, most challenging one yet.

8

AN UNEXPECTED TRANSITION

My decision to leave NASA's Jet Propulsion Laboratory 10 years earlier provided me with opportunities beyond the privilege of working in the aerospace industry. I learned that my residency at the "Outpatient Clinic" was an exciting manifestation of how God is able to help us to accomplish quality work with integrity and excellence while being ministers of the Gospel in the workplace.

At AVCO we attempted to live with the changes in the industry, but it was not clear as to how we could survive as a space technology group when the projected government forecasts were so very pessimistic. Meanwhile, I was given an opportunity to explore employment opportunities with other companies in the area.

At the same time, my family and I were involved with Grace Chapel, a large, dynamic, growing congregation only a few miles from home. Dr. Gordon MacDonald, the senior pastor and I had known each other for a few years. He was exploring the idea of providing training for lay people who, like me, were in the community and the workplace. We had such conversations in the past, and he wondered if I had any interest in training others in what I had learned. I did express interest and Agape Fellowship was formed, a ministry where believers could learn how to share their faith in a natural way at work and in the neighborhood.

Unrelated to that class, however, my pastor asked if I would be willing to talk with a couple struggling in their marriage. I agreed and met with them several times. Those meetings revealed to me a new and satisfying purpose as I continued my engineering career.

In the meantime, at a monthly meeting of the local chapter of the Institute of Electrical and Electronic Engineers, I met the head of the antenna department at MIT's Lincoln Laboratory. We were chatting about my experiences in spacecraft antenna design at JPL and then at AVCO. He then mentioned an opening at the lab for an engineer and suggested I submit an application. I did so and was invited to an on-site interview for the position. One week later, I received an invitation to join the team at Lincoln Labs. The feelings I had when I received an offer to leave JPL for AVCO resurfaced. Another test of faith was emerging, only this time the stakes were even higher.

About the same time, I received another call from my pastor who wanted me to know that the couple he referred to me had decided to make a new start and work on their marriage relationship. Moreover, they had appreciated my willingness to help them. Then Pastor MacDonald said "Who knows Dick, maybe next year at this time you won't be an engineer anymore." I hesitated in my response outwardly but inwardly his words fell on me like thunder! I had been thinking and wondering for several months if God's call on my life would one day lead in a whole new direction. However, I really couldn't think about it now. I had work to do, but the seed was sown and the clock was ticking. I confided in John that I had received an invitation to join Lincoln Labs but that it was complicated by another offer, which presented the possibility of a total change of direction in my career, which I could not ignore,. He was not surprised and said he would support me in wherever God was calling me.

A few months later I met with my pastor, who told me that he had met with the elders of the congregation, to explore the possibility of calling me to the full time position of Minister of Evangelism and Discipleship at the church. They agreed, and included in the offer was reimbursement for theological training at Gordon Theological Seminary which was within commuting distance of the church.

So with the future of the spacecraft antenna systems group at AVCO threatened by lack of government support, and with an offer to join a prestigious organization like Lincoln Labs, and the opportunity to say no to both options and enter Christian ministry full time, my faith was being challenged like never before. I fell back on one of my favorite texts of Scripture which had guided me in the past and would do so in the days to come; the wisdom of Proverbs.

"Trust in the LORD with all your heart and lean not on your own understanding; in all your ways submit to him and he will make your paths straight" (Prov. 3:5-6).

I learned early in my Christian life that God does not take responsibility from us, but asks us to place our trust and faith in Him. So decisions are ours, but the wisdom that guides those decisions comes from Him. His promise is that while we decide by faith, He will make the path straight as we walk before Him.

In the end, I had the support of my faithful wife and two young boys who were praying with me that God would lead us into the future. While our faith was strong that He was leading, I had one unspoken question; how could we live on a totally different level of income? In reality, we knew that if God was calling, He would provide. God was our provider and we had many years of experience with Him guiding us in all areas of our lives. In retrospect, concerning the new ministry opportunity, money never became an issue; it was no more than a passing thought for both Kathy and me.

We had been in prayer concerning the upcoming decision, but we wanted our ten and eight year old boys, Mark and Erik to feel a part of the decision. One day at breakfast Kathy said, "Boys, what do you think of Dad maybe leaving engineering and becoming a pastor?" Without hesitation they responded with enthusiastic thumbs up! We wanted to make this decision as a family and move through the transition together. The boys with their child-like faith were an encouragement to us. We continued to pray.

Back at AVCO, the pressure was mounting to make a decision. A few colleagues, who knew what I was wrestling with, were wondering what I was going to do with the offer from Lincoln Labs. I became somewhat distant from it all and buried myself in the work before me. Lincoln Labs was waiting for my answer, as were John and my pastor. It was decision time. After much prayer and counsel from trusted friends, I decided to leave my beloved career, for which I had spent much time in education and thoroughly enjoyed, to follow Jesus into the church to use me in a totally different way. The peace which passes all understanding was there, as it had been in decisions of the past.

I called Kathy to let her know how I felt and what I had decided. She was in agreement. Then I called my pastor and told him that I had come to a decision to leave my engineering career and join the staff at Grace Chapel as their minister of Evangelism and Discipleship. Finally, I went to John and told him that I had made a decision for a career change, and was going into ministry full time with the encouragement of my church. He was fully supportive and we agreed on a date for my departure.

Trying to explain to my co-workers that I had decided not to accept the offer with Lincoln Labs was further proof to some that I had lost my mind. I called Lincoln Laboratories and thanked them for the opportunity to join their staff, but let them know that I had decided respectfully, to refuse the invitation realizing that I was turning down a premier offer to work with the best. I tried to explain the unexplainable; that I was leaving my career in engineering to enter Christian ministry and serve in the church full time.

I went home that day with assurance for what I believed was the right decision. Again, it was that same peace that settled in my mind and heart when years before I decided to leave JPL and sunny Southern California to move to the East Coast to join AVCO. As a family we thanked God for how He had used us in years past. Before leaving however, there was someone in the "Outpatient Clinic" who had been looking for a resolution to the emptiness of his own life.

LAST DAYS AS AN ENGINEER

My final weeks at AVCO were a time of finishing reports and projects. John had agreed to take over the Bible study group, which had been operating for a few years. It was hard to say goodbye to those with whom I gathered week after week to study God's word in the middle of a work day. Sermons From Science, sponsored by the Bible study group, was a satisfying experience.

On my last day, I made the rounds to say good-bye to men and women with whom I had worked over the years. One of the company directors wanted to know what interested me in this "thing" called ministry. In the end, he affirmed me and stated that if things didn't work out, even ten years later, if I called him he would re-hire me. I thought that was gracious of him.

As I passed the office of the Vice President of Engineering, Harvey Brown, I thought I should stop and let him know that it was my last day. I did not know Harvey that well and only saw him at occasional meetings where business opportunities consistent with our expertise were being discussed. The door to his office was closed so I knocked lightly, and heard the words "come in." I stuck my head in the door and said, "Harvey, I was just passing by and wanted to say goodbye, as today is my last day at AVCO." "So I hear," he said, "come on in, shut the door, have a seat." I closed the door behind me, approached his big oak desk and sat down. I had not been in his office but a few times over the years, and its design reflected that of a company vice president. Harvey continued, "I have heard that you are leaving the company, but the thing I don't understand is that you are changing careers and going into some kind of ministry you call it? What is that all about and how did you come to that decision?"

I explained briefly the change that had taken place in my life years before I studied for a career in engineering. I shared with him how I had wandered aimlessly in life, experiencing personal suffering before finding the answer for my being here on earth in the person of Jesus Christ. I then told him about my recent visit with my pastor at Grace Chapel in Lexington, who offered me an opportunity to start a new career as a pastor serving on the Grace Chapel staff.

Quite abruptly, Harvey interrupted me and said, "Dick, you would think that I am a successful person, wouldn't you?" I responded in the affirmative by referring to the many plaques and awards that adorned his wall, representing recognition from

NASA and other government agencies. I said, "It seems to me that, yes, your reputation here at the company indicates success, and the awards on your wall confirm it." Then pointing with his right hand and tapping his heart, he said, "No, I am not successful because I am not successful in here. How do I get what you have?" I knew what he was asking and reached for the New Testament which I had in my pocket. As I opened it, I asked him for permission to read from it. I read passages from the claims of Jesus as the Son of God, and the Apostles who declared that the problem of sin was overcome through faith in Jesus' death and resurrection. I told Harvey that God sent His only Son into the world in order to provide a mid-course correction for us. I explained that Jesus had come to heal unsuccessful hearts and help us to turn away from personal sin. By inviting the spirit of Jesus to fill his heart, he would know the peace that Jesus promised.

Over his big desk, I extended an invitation to him to receive the Lord Jesus into his 'unsuccessful heart' for the forgiveness of his sin. I volunteered to lead him through a prayer and he agreed that I do so. He cupped his head in his hands over his desk and we prayed. When we finished I said, "Harvey, you just asked the Son of God to enter your life by faith, is that right?" He said yes. He affirmed that there was a new sense of peace in his heart! I then told him that the peace of God is one of the first signs that God gives to us when we invite Him into our very being and proof that our sins have been forgiven. I continued to share from the Scriptures the promises of God for all those with faith in his Son. I read from 1 John which tells us that we can "know", that we have eternal life. This was the first scripture I read, after my own spiritual transformation many years earlier.

"I write these things to you who believe in the name of the Son of God so that you may know that you have eternal life" (1 John 5:13).

I encouraged Harvey to establish a daily practice of reading from God's word and practicing intimacy with God through prayer. Harvey thanked me for stopping by and wished me well. I thanked him for taking the time to talk. As I approached the door and opened it to leave he said, while wagging his finger in the air, "Dick, this is the most important day of my whole life." I smiled and said I was glad I stopped in.

I went back to John's office and shared the experience I just had with Harvey. John said, "You're kidding, right?" I said "No! Talk with him and invite him to the Bible study." It was John who had previously indicated that he had seen Harvey at a few of the Sermon from Science films in the auditorium. I learned a few months later that Harvey had taken a new Vice President position at a West Coast aerospace company and found a theological school which offered lay persons evening courses in the Bible. My experience with Harvey was just another confirmation that in the workplace people at all levels of responsibility desire to interact with followers of Jesus who have no agenda except love, and are willing to share the good news of the Gospel.

As I walked back to my office, I was thinking about that sign on the building which I had seen above the entrance doors almost ten years earlier -"Outpatient Clinic". I now understood clearly that God knew of those who were looking for Him, although they did not know how to find Him. Nevertheless, He was in the workplace every day, seeking them out, and offering them His peace. Through the daily relationships of working together at a common task, some of my colleagues found that peace. I picked up some remaining personal items, shook hands with a few other colleagues, and left the building for home and a new career; a topic for a future memoir of my life in the local church.

EPILOGUE

I have written a faithful account of a life that was rescued from the power of death and which, by the grace of God, rose to allow evidence that God is merciful, desirous of us, and faithful to all He has promised.

With salvation come spiritual gifts or graces that are given to each follower of Jesus by the sovereign choice of God. I found from the beginning that somehow, when I shared what God did in my life; many people responded and desired a relationship with Him. I take no credit for the response of those who have found spiritual life through what I shared with them. Other believers have other kinds of gifts, and all gifts are given to accomplish the purposes of God among men, which are to serve others, sharing with them the "hope that is within you" (1 Peter 3:15).

I learned, shortly after receiving this new life in myself, that untold numbers of people have empty hearts originally created to be the dwelling place of God Himself. As a follower of Jesus, there would be people in my life for whom I might be the only contact for the Gospel message. Would I be able to communicate God's love in such a way that they would become followers of Jesus?

God revealed to me that I was not to trust being logical, or to answer every question, but to be ready to give testimony concerning the hope that I have within (1 Peter 3:15). Jesus indicated that we were to be light so that the message might be seen or sensed in us, before it be explained. Without any evidence that my life had been touched by God, I would in vain try to persuade others of what I knew to be true. How that evidence becomes known or seen by others, I don't know. It's something the Holy Spirit does when we are available to Him for the sake of others.

Ministry in the workplace, regardless of one's spiritual gifts, is the privilege of all followers of Jesus. In my journey, I have met others who have quietly radiated the Holy Spirit and given testimony of Jesus through their lives. I am grateful to God for the lives that were touched by the light of the Holy Spirit in this unlikely servant, laboring in the "Outpatient Clinic" of the workplace. Indeed, for them, the light pierced their darkness.

HOW TO CONTACT THE AUTHOR

A dditional copies of this book may be purchased by contacting the author at the email address below:

piercinglightmemoir@gmail.com

The book is also available on Amazon.com under the author's name Richard E. Herskind or the book title *When Light Pierced the Darkness – An Extraordinary Journey of Redemption* published by 5 Stones Publishing Company. The paperback version is available for $14.00 plus tax and S&H.

Please note that Richard is available for speaking at Churches, to church groups, and conferences helping believers to expect God to use them to attract colleagues to faith in Jesus Christ, in their places of work.